The 1940s *Look*

RECREATING THE FASHIONS, HAIR STYLES AND MAKE-UP OF THE SECOND WORLD WAR

Books are to be returned on or before
the last date below.

www.librex.co.uk

This Month's SPECIAL THREE-IN-ONE PATTERN

Looking Forward To Sunny Days

Thanks

I would like to take this opportunity to thank the following people: my old friend Steve Cole for his help with spectacles, the College of Optometrists, and especially their librarian, Ms. J Ayres. Also Gordon Ayres (no relation), for the loan of period magazines for sourcing illustrations.

John Skinner for the art work, and our designer Annie Falconer-Gronow, who has done a superb job to a very tight deadline.

Ian Bayley, who has aged five years in our one-year project, my wife Carol Harris whose comments, though not always welcomed, have always been useful; and to our families, Jan, Michael and Charlotte, and William and Ralph, who have had to put up with us.

First published in the United Kingdom in 2006
Reprinted 2007, 2009 by
Sabrestorm Publishing
90, Lennard Road, Dunton Green,
Sevenoaks, Kent TN13 2UX

www.sabrestorm.com

Mike Brown has asserted the moral right to be identified as the author of this work.

British Library Cataloguing in Publication Data
A catalogue record for this book is available from the British Library

Designed and typeset by Annie Falconer-Gronow
Artwork by John Skinner

ISBN: 978-0-9552723-1-8

Printed by Tien Wah Press

The 1940s Look

RECREATING THE FASHIONS, HAIR STYLES AND MAKE-UP OF THE SECOND WORLD WAR

Mike Brown

SABRESTORM

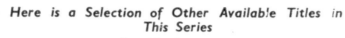

CONTENTS

CLOTHING

INTRODUCTION

The inter-war period had seen a rapid rise in the quality of clothing worn by the average Briton. During the 1930s, Jewish tailors and cutters who arrived as refugees from Germany and Austria, brought with them ways of cutting patterns that ensured better fitting ready-to-wear garments. Improved methods of mass production meant that the quality and range of off-the-peg clothing was far higher than pre-First World War, while prices had fallen. Made-to-measure clothes still remained the province of the better-off, but those less well-off could afford to buy off-the-peg more often, and as such, take more interest in what was fashionable.

The outbreak of war brought strident calls that the nation take on the mantle of the puritans; all forms of entertainment should cease, and such fripperies as new clothes, hair styles and make-up should be regarded as unpatriotic. But this did not last for long as people appreciated the importance of good morale. After a brief time, much returned to normal, including fashion; true, much of it was war-oriented, the gas-mask curl was introduced for women's hair (for keeping hair neat under the respirator), and their clothes took on a military air, while for many young men the military look was a more enforced one, albeit at the government's expense.

◀ A range of women's and children's clothing, including the WVS uniform of the lady kneeling (centre).

"Latest thing in blackout fashions is a white patent leather waistcoat"

In the first few months of the war, with the blackout in mind, people responded to government exhortations to 'wear something white at night' in various ways. The newspapers suggested items such as white hat bands and belts, and manufacturers offered 'luminous' articles, including buttons, arm-bands, and artificial flower button-holes, most of which did not work. The **Daily Mirror** in September 1939 reported the 'latest thing in blackout fashions is a white patent leather waistcoat'. However, most people, if they bothered at all, contented themselves with carrying a newspaper, or, cheapest of all, men pulled their shirt-tails out, which, being longer than their coats,

▾ A Government poster from early in the war urging the public to wear something white to be seen in the blackout.
(Crown Copyright)

did the job perfectly well.

As the Phoney War turned to Blitzkrieg, things changed again. In July 1940, the Chancellor, Sir Kingsley Wood, introduced his budget, raising income tax to 8s 6d in the pound. He appealed for personal economies, including in dress: 'It may be, that in a few months, when people walk along wearing a shabby suit, or a shabby hat, the remark will be made, "He is a patriotic man carrying out the Chancellor's idea".'

The editor of **The Tailor and Cutter** disagreed: *'A shabby suit is not a badge of patriotism ... it is a clear indication of the wearer's general slackness, his loss of personal pride and his adoption of the don't care attitude. Surely the last thing to be encouraged in these days.'*

Over the next few months a scarcity of raw materials and the needs of the military led to government restrictions on the amount and styles of clothing a manufacturer could produce. This meant that many produced only their more expensive and most profitable lines, and the government was forced to bring in the Utility scheme to keep prices down.

Later things changed again when rationing was introduced. Lack of goods in the shops, coupled with high employment, meant that many people had more to spend than ever before; if rationing meant you could only get one overcoat or suit every three or four years, it had better be one which would last well, and expense was, for many, a secondary consideration.

Yet the gap between the richest and the poorest was still far greater than today. When we look at clothes of the period these differences have to be remembered. Much of what we describe refers to the better-off working class and the middle classes; the poorer and older sections of the community would not have paid so much attention to the fashions of the time.

When walking after dark to-night

For safety's sake wear something

WHITE

MEN

Men's fashions changed very slowly at this time. Most men wore clothes which had changed very little from those worn by their fathers, the basic outfit being the three-piece lounge suit, shirt with detachable 'soft' collar, tie and hat.

The suit was the central plank of men's dress. Every so often, depending on how well-off you were, a suit would be bought, either second-hand, new off-the-peg, or if you could afford it, made-to-measure. This suit would be your 'Sunday best' and as the name implies, it would be worn for church, or for formal occasions such as weddings, funerals, Christmas day, and so on. Your previous Sunday best, by now a little worn, would become your everyday suit, and if your 'rotation period' was short enough, and your previous everyday suit still wearable, this would be used for work if you had a manual job, or for gardening, decorating, or other jobs around the house. For some, however, the time for buying a new Sunday best was when your everyday suit had become too disreputable for further wear.

▸ A hand-knitted, v-necked sweater. As the war progressed, and wool became difficult to get hold of, fairisle became more common as a way of using odd bits of wool.

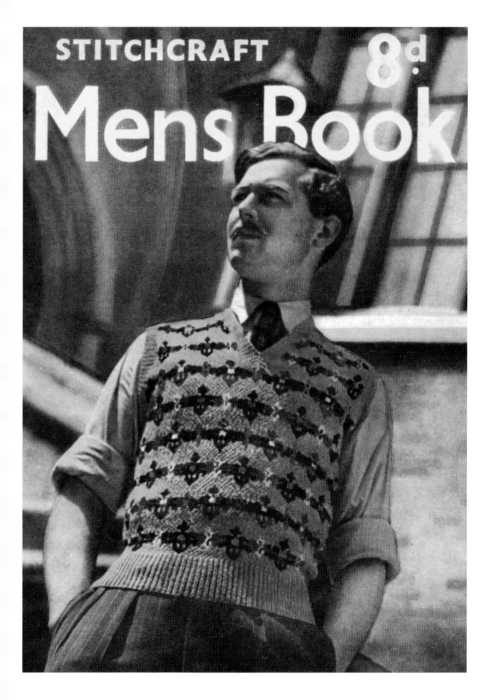

STITCHCRAFT 8d
Mens Book

Of course, the three pieces of a suit did not all wear at the same rate. The trousers usually went first, and new suits were often sold with the option of two pairs of trousers to counter this. Next would go the jacket, and finally the waistcoat. For this reason, men in 'casual' or work dress are often seen with mis-matching trousers, waistcoat and jacket.

Having just one or two suits to be worn for all sorts of occasions meant that they tended to be fairly conservative in colour. Dark blues, greys, browns and blacks, often with fine pin-stripes were by far the most common colours, and wool and serge the likeliest materials. There were some exceptions to this rule. Many clerical workers still wore the traditional black jacket and waistcoat, with grey pin-stripe trousers; these were known as 'blackcoat' jobs, in the same way as we talk of 'blue-collar' workers. In rural areas, tweed suits were the norm, often three-piece, optionally with plus-fours; the lounge suit sometimes being termed the 'town suit'.

Jackets, somewhat shorter in length than is fashionable today, overwhelmingly had wide, 'wing' lapels, with square cut, padded shoulders, and were markedly rounded at the bottom of the front. Tweed jackets, or 'sports' jackets, similar in style to suit jackets but in more 'racey' colours and checks, might be worn for weekends or holidays.

Other casual jackets included the 'windjammer' – a waist-length jacket, fastened with buttons or a zip, usually in suede, suedette, corduroy or leather, with a shirt-type collar, two low front pouch pockets, and elastic welts at cuffs and waist.

▸ Good examples of the range of shirt collars in use, and of the popular trilby hat. (Crown Copyright)

(top right) Austin Reed advert from March 1940, showing the main variations in suit styling: collars, single and double breasted, and square and round cut fronts. Note the older man on the left wearing the less fashionable suit. Compare this with the 'demob' suit on page 8.

(bottom right) A typical knitted sports shirt of the period worn by both men and women.

Trousers were roomy in the leg and long in the crotch, and fastened with buttons. Even though the zip or 'zipp' had been around for some time and was used extensively for women's skirts, men were, understandably, wary of possible accidents. Although some casual trousers were supplied with belt loops, button-fastening elastic braces were almost universal, and it seems strange to us today that the major areas of wear on men's shirts were in the pit of the back due to the rubbing of the 'Y' piece of the braces, and a 'V' at the front caused by the top of the waistcoat. Casual trousers, for summer or sports, were in the same style as suit trousers, normally in white or grey flannel, worsted or tweed. There were plus-fours, but these were largely restricted to the well-off and mainly seen on the golf course or at shooting parties. One of the few areas subject to fashion was the question of turn-ups (or not) on trousers. By 1939 the swing had been to turn-ups and remained so until austerity provisions decreed otherwise in March 1942.

Everyday shirts were worn with detachable collars held on with collar studs. Shirts were normally sold with two collars, which could also be bought separately. There were many styles of collar, from the very formal, stiff, winged collar; stiff, round collars, or the more fashionable soft, short or long pointed collar; the latter, somewhat longer in the point than worn today, being the most fashionable. Sleeves were long (held up with elastic arm-bands), and wide, usually with turned-over cuffs, often fastened with cuff-links. Shirt-tails were much longer than today, reaching almost to the knees, and most shirts only opened to mid-chest level. Stripes of varying widths were common.

To wear a shirt without its collar was only socially acceptable when doing heavy manual work, such as gardening or in industry (although many chose to wear one even then) or at home. Only the coarsest man would go out, or receive guests at home, without first putting on his collar and tie. It is often surprising to see photographs of workers in heavy industry or the building trade wearing waistcoats and ties. There was also the 'sports-shirt', similar to a normal shirt, but with a fixed

CLOTHING TERMS

Rotation period	Sunday best	Casual
Wind-jammer	Blackcoat	Racey
Town suit	Wing collar	Choker

collar, worn outside the jacket, without a tie, at the beach or when hiking or on similar informal occasions, as was a short-sleeved, usually machine-knitted shirt, of the type later called a 'Fred Perry'. A cardigan or pullover would often be worn as a casual alternative to the waistcoat.

Ties were the splash of colour in an otherwise conservative outfit. They were usually much shorter than today's versions, as they were worn with waistcoats or cardigans and therefore only needed to reach half way down the chest. This could result in the tie 'breaking loose' from under the waistcoat; to avoid this, they were often anchored with tie-pins. Bow ties were worn, but were seen as either very formal, or a little eccentric. Cravats were worn only by the better-off as part of summer dress.

Overcoats were large and thick, often of tweed or wool, normally with a belt, and with collars of the same style as on jackets. Mackintoshes, or raincoats were popular, especially 'trench coats' named after the style of raincoat popular amongst officers in the Great War. Overcoats might be worn with a 'choker'; a cotton, rayon or silk scarf, usually about

12 inches by 48, worn either crossed over inside the overcoat or tied in a loose knot round the throat. This was a style popular with the working-class. In really cold weather, a knitted scarf might be worn, as might a cardigan or pullover, sometimes under the waistcoat.

These were the common styles of dress worn by most men during the late thirties and in essence remained the style of men's dress throughout the war. Some changes would be introduced, mainly as a result of Board of Trade restrictions and austerity measures, yet by 1945 little had changed that much.

Clothes rationing was introduced with no forewarning – to avoid panic buying – on June 1, 1941. In his radio speech announcing rationing, Oliver Lyttelton, President of the Board of Trade, said: *I know all the women will look smart, but we men may look shabby. If we do we must not be ashamed. In war the term "battle-stained" is an honourable one.'*

Everyone over four years old was to receive 66 clothing coupons for the first year; later, children and workers in certain industries would receive extras, and the annual amount of coupons would fall, but sexual equality in this, at least, would remain.

▲ ▶ A selection of men's ties from the period. Diagonal stripes were very fashionable while tartans, checks and polka dots were all popular.

A four-year plan for a man's wardrobe, from **Sew & Save**

First year
1 pair boots or shoes
6 pairs socks
1 suit (no waistcoat)
1 overcoat
Collars, ties or handkerchiefs

Second year
1 pair boots or shoes
6 pairs socks
1 pair corduroy trousers
3 shirts (silk or cotton)
2 pairs of pants
2 vests
1 pair gloves

Third year
1 pair boots or shoes
5 pairs socks
1 suit
1 pullover
2 pairs of pyjamas

Fourth year
1 pair boots or shoes
6 pairs socks
1 overcoat, or unlined mackintosh and vests
3 shirts
2 pairs of pants
Collars, ties or handkerchiefs.

The Board of Trade survey into how people used their coupons cast an interesting light on men's wardrobes. During the first year of rationing, men spent 26 per cent of their coupons on shirts and underwear (roughly, two shirts and one set of combinations) 17 per cent on boots and shoes (roughly two and a half pairs) 15 per cent on socks (roughly three pairs) and 22 per cent on suits, jackets and trousers (actually less than one suit, or two to three pairs of trousers). The remaining 20 per cent had to cover all other requirements. During the second year these proportions remained substantially unchanged, apart from a fall in the percentage spent on suits, jackets and trousers. Over the first three years the average man bought one suit (without a waistcoat), and three pairs of trousers.

In August 1941 the Board of Trade prohibited the production of men's double-breasted suits and permanent turn-ups on trousers. Trousers too long in the leg had to be turned up, however, rather than cut to length, to avoid wasting material, and it was

◄ The cardigan, worn with the almost compulsory pipe. Notice the very long shirt collar.

▸ A 'demob' suit.
The shirt is being worn
without a tie, with the
collar typically worn
outside the jacket.

▸ (opposite) A hand-
knitted, polo-neck
sweater, used for sport
or leisure activities.

then president of the Board of Trade, replied caustically: *'There can be no equality of sacrifice in this war. Some must lose life and limbs, others only the turn-ups on their trousers.'*

In January 1944, the Board announced that since plans were being made to provide suits 'of normal peacetime design' to men demobilised from the Forces, it would be impractical to retain restrictions on suits designed for the general pubic, and the coupon-value of 'austerity' suits would be reduced to clear stocks. One of the big changes in style of these 'demob' suits was the bottom of the front of the jacket, which was now square-cut.

Many of the men returning from the Forces found their old clothes no longer fitted them. Regular food and exercise had changed their shape for the better. Some did not have the chance to find out if they still fitted; they had been used to make do and mend by their wife in the intervening period. I have spoken to several men who came home to find their wardrobes completely empty!

It was pointed out in the book **Sew & Save** that, as most men's clothes were almost impossible to re-make at home, they should be kept in a state of good repair so as to last longer. Shirts were usually the main problem, although work could be done on them. Apart from the areas already mentioned, the main place of wear was the cuff. These, the book pointed out, could be 'turned':

'To turn a cuff, unpick it carefully at the wrist-edge with a needle and a pair of small, sharp scissors to pull the stitches away. When you have detached the cuff, seam it along close to the edge just below the frayed part, then turn it inside-out so that the frayed edge is now inside, and press it. Attach the cuff once more to the wrist-band by neatly hemming down either side, taking care to keep the gathers or pleats in the same position.' **Sew & Save.**

not uncommon for tailors to cut suit trousers too long, so that a turn-up would have to be put in. The Board further limited the amount of stitching permitted in a suit, and placed a limit on the number of buttons used. The tails of men's shirts were to be shorter, and pockets in a man's jacket limited to three, in waist-coats to two and in trousers, three. In 1943, pyjama pockets were banned but this regula-tion was overturned the following year.

The conservatism in dress which had kept men's fashions fairly stable also meant that men reacted far more strongly than women to the effects of austerity regulations. There was even parliamentary pressure to have the ban on trouser turn-ups overturned. Hugh Dalton,

The tails of men's shirts were to be shorter, and pockets in a man's jacket limited to three

Patches for other parts of a shirt, such as the neck, could be made using pieces cut from the tail, and the hole filled in with a piece of cotton or a piece from an older shirt.

While pattern books included instructions for knitted ties and hand-made shirts, home-made clothes for men were usually jumpers, socks, and scarves. Scarves could be hand-made from 1/4 yard of 36-inch wide material, and fringed at the ends. A winter scarf used fine plain or check wool, and little tassels might be made to go on the ends. To make these, wool should be wound round a cardboard gauge about half-a-dozen times, as you don't want them too thick.

Most male workers in industry wore overalls, either of the bib-and-brace, all-in-one type, or long coat styles. Heavy working shirts were produced to go with overalls, but many wore ordinary shirts. When rationing was first introduced some industrial overalls, such as boiler suits, were coupon-free. The result, not surprisingly, was that these garments were widely purchased for ordinary domestic use, to save wear on precious 'good clothes'. This loophole was soon closed; instead arrangements were made to supply overalls to industrial workers at low coupon-rates, covered by the issue of ten extra coupons to nearly all industrial and agricultural workers. Workers in the heaviest industries could apply for extra coupons from a small hardship pool.

Most workers in offices or retail jobs continued to wear lounge suits, while the use of 'blackcoat' outfits diminished in most jobs for want of coupons. People who worked outside usually wore heavy trousers, with shirt, waistcoat and jacket, and in cold weather chunky sweaters, often of the polo-neck variety.

Men's underwear was almost exclusively white, and fell into two categories: the summer version, comprising a sleeveless singlet and shorts, and the winter version with a long or short-sleeved vest and 'long johns'. Normally wartime shorts or long johns would have no

elastic but had tape-loops at the top to coincide with the braces; the shirt would be tucked in to the pants, and the braces attached to the trousers through the tapes on the pants, thus keeping them up. The latest thing in underpants were Y-fronts. Their adverts claimed that they were 'scientifically styled', gave 'masculine support' and 'no gaping' while needing 'no buttons, no ironing'. They came in two types: shorts, which we would now think of as trunks, and 'midways', rather like boxer shorts with tight legs. Interestingly, a national survey by Mass Observation at this time found that men possessed, on average, one pair of underpants – which suggests that many did not wear pants at all.

Many poorer men and women wore their underclothes to bed, and it was not uncommon on cold nights to wear that day's shirt (minus collar). Where special nightwear was worn, it was still common in 1939 for this to be a nightshirt, often called a gaffer nightshirt. This was similar in design to a day shirt, but with longer tails. The onset of war, or more specifically the air raid warning, pushed many men over to pyjamas – they did not want the neighbours to see their bare legs as they made their way to the garden shelter!

'It was known that the King had put away white tie and tails for the duration. His subjects who still attended formal occasions mostly contented themselves with soft collar and shirt, but magazine photographs show tails being worn long after the fall of France.' (**The Phoney War on the Home Front**.)

On the whole, men's formal dress, like that of the King, was uniform, either of the Forces and the Home Guard, or civilian bodies like Civil Defence; or, for those with no uniform to wear, the lounge suit, or in extremis, the dinner jacket. When such occasions arose which would warrant the wearing of formal dress, hire shops, such as Moss Bros., would supply the necessary.

WOMEN

'When you feel tired of your old clothes remember that by making them do you are contributing some part of an aeroplane, a gun or a tank.' Oliver Lyttelton, President of the Board of Trade, in his radio broadcast introducing clothing rationing in June 1941.

As the prospect of war loomed, military styling became fashionable – epaulettes, military-style jackets and brass buttons were popular. The government bought up all available supplies of wool cloth, which would be needed for service uniforms.

It wasn't long before fashion writers began to give advice on what to wear in wartime: *'Don't go about in defeatist garments – shabby-collared coats, hats which have wilted, frocks which you had every intention of discarding a few months ago.'* Several advised that, to get rid of gloom brought on by the war, women should cheer themselves up by going through their wardrobes and having a grand clear-out of all their unwanted clothes. How many who took

▼ Dresses from February 1940. Note the below-knee length, the puffed sleeves, and the snood worn by the woman on the right.

3256   2943   3252

▲ The two-piece suit became an important part of women's dress, giving as it did three variations – a suit, a skirt, and a jacket.

▸ Illustration from 1940. As clothes became harder to get, the idea of mix-and-match boomed as a way of stretching out a limited wardrobe.

this advice would regret it when rationing was introduced less than two years later?

The situation called for a sartorial response. In autumn 1939, the **Home Companion** advised: '*If you're lucky enough to possess a fur coat, short or long, you'll wear it as it's never been worn before – running down cold passages, trotting round the house to make sure that your blackout is satisfactory, covering your autumn suit.*'

The alternative was to make out of fur fabric: '*one of those chic little coatees which are perfect to wear over woollen frocks ... Make it very simple in style, and roomy. So that it will slip over extra woollies.*'

A long dressing gown was 'a necessity' if you were going to have to spring up from a warm bed at the sound of the air-raid warning, especially for those who wore nightdresses in preference to pyjamas. For best service in the shelter, this dressing gown should fasten right up to the throat and have a hood; the alternative being to attach a warm hood of thick woollen material to a collarless dressing gown or coat.

With thousands of men being called up, fashion dictated that women wore something that would not clash with their partner's uniform. The **Daily Mirror** of September 13, 1939 reported: '*Special colours to go with khaki are already being experimented with ... Purplish wines*

will predominate and there is a new colour, Manchu Brown, that will tone splendidly with Army Khaki.*'

There was for a while a fashion war between those who declared that it was a woman's duty to look as glamorous as possible for themselves and the morale of the men going to war, and those who thought that war required a fitting austerity of dress. In the end common-sense and compromise prevailed: '*If you want to be in the fashion – be simple. Avoid elaborate jewellery and fol-de-rols. Wear long-sleeved dresses for parties rather than the décolleté variety. Make for a tailored coat rather with brightly coloured scarves at the neck than fur collars and such.*' **Home Notes**, December 1939.

Clothes prices began to rise very early in the war, while the government's austerity provisions limited the choices available. These austerity provisions forbade among other things the use of embroidery, and of appliqué work and lace on lingerie. They placed limits on the depth of hems and on the number of seams allowed in garments of different kinds, restricted the use of tucks, pleats and buttons, and prohibited the use of velvet, fur, fur fabric and some other materials for the trimming of women's coats and jackets.

Government limitations on production meant shortages. Women looked for alternative sources of clothing even before rationing. One lay in the hundreds of thousands of men now in the forces, whose wardrobes stood like Aladdin's caves, full of possibilities.

Woman magazine of February 1940 suggested: '*Now that feminine clothes are so much simpler and crisper we've no need to imitate men's fashions. We can just beg, borrow or steal them from the boy friend and wear them just exactly as they are. You couldn't have anything more utterly charming and gay than his pert little bow [tie] under your chin.*

'*The slickness of crisp snowy white against a dusky background, the smartness of a tailored starched waistcoat, with the latest deep-cut V-shaped front and waistcoat points – you get all these from his evening white waistcoat. And if he won't lend you his own precious waistcoat buttons buy some large pearl*

twice one is THREE!

It's an economy to make up these two WOMAN patterns – for they combine to form a third and very useful outfit

3351

3428

3351

3428

NOBODY these days is bothering about having a great number of clothes—the ideal thing is to possess a few good outfits that can be juggled with to give infinite variety to your wardrobe.

A different jacket to contrast with your skirt, one or two extra blouses— these are the things that can change the whole nature of one serviceable suit.

One frock will be the back-bone of your wardrobe and you can wear it over and over again with continued success, if you slip over it the jacket of your suit and wear it occasionally as a two-piece.

This game of change partners with your frocks is the secret of successful dressing, especially in these days when we must all make one outfit do the work of two or three.

But to achieve the best effects, your basic frocks and suits must have good simple lines.

Look at the two patterns we're giving you this week, and see how one smart suit and a warm winter frock can be expanded into three elegant and separate outfits.

PATTERN 3351. It's as neat and perfectly tailored as any suit you could find, and it's got quite the newest kind of built-in pockets. Made up in a smooth dark cloth or in a tweed, it could be adapted for either town or country wear. It comes in bust sizes 30-38. Size 34 takes $2\frac{7}{8}$ yd. 54-in. material. Pattern price 1s., post free.

PATTERN 3428. Here's a dress that could be infinitely useful throughout the winter. Entirely without trimming of any kind, it might be made up in a patterned wool and worn very successfully with the jacket of Pattern 3351 to form a third and very attractive outfit. The frock comes in bust sizes 30-38. Size 34 takes $2\frac{7}{8}$ yd. 54-in. material. Pattern price 9d., post free.

buttons and sew them on instead. *That bold sporting check suit he fancies himself in so much has a waist-coat he probably scarcely uses. Why not knit him a pullover and borrow the waistcoat for yourself? It will look grand slipped over a jumper or shirt, or worn in the country over a frock or with a suit.*

'*Borrow one of his stiff collars and wear it on your plainest, darkest dress.*'

This early foray on men's wardrobes was to become a full-scale attack as rationing and shortages hit home.

With the fall of France in June 1940, the main focus for fashion inspiration shifted to America. As the war continued, and more and more articles were added to the list of those things 'gone but not forgotten', America, through the glamour of Hollywood, became a sort of paradise, and fashion writers spoke of America as they had once spoken of Paris: *The smart American clothes of this winter have combined knitting with fabric. Not only will a suit jacket have knitted sleeves and yoke, but even full-length coats have a waistcoat effect worked in stitch knitting.*' **Woman and Home**, December 1940.

On June 1, 1941, came rationing. Jacqueline Meriot wrote in the **Sunday Pictorial**:

'*I predict that startling new styles, a blend of common-sense and ingenuity, will soon appear on the promenades as a result of the clothes rationing order.*

'*Summer stockings will be shed to conserve our meagre ration for the winter. Painted legs will doubt-less set off our many-coloured Joseph coats, fashioned from bits and pieces of varied hues. ... Pyjama jackets will be used as blouses to introduce a tunic with a Russian air.*

'*Dresses will be renovated one with the other. Blue backs will be stitched over worn black ones. Red tops will be fitted to plaid skirts. Worn sleeves will be replaced in bright colours.*'

She was, of course, pretty accurate, though her predictions for men were far less so.

▲ With shortages and rationing, men's clothes became a useful resource for women. Here a man's stiff collar is looking very good with a turban.

◄ A man's 'sporty' waistcoat is here pressed into service by his other half.

Woman magazine of October 1941 gave directions for the best choice of frock, coat and suit:

'A short sleeved day-length frock has so many possibilities, it will take you anywhere from a social to a cinema, from a tea-party to a dance. It should be in a plain colour so you will not tire of it so quickly as if it were patterned. Moreover, if you buy your new frock in a light colour and you choose a material that will dye, you should be able to change its colour more than once.'

They suggested: *'a simple style with no complicated pleating, insertion or embroideries to get out of order or to wear out, so it will last you a long while and will not date. And on a plain frock of this kind you can put all sorts of clever additions to freshen it up. You can put a new lace collar fitting over the crêpe one. You can wear two big jewelled clips at the throat, or add contrasting collar and cuffs or a fashionable necklet.'*

Next: *'One coat must do duty for both town and country in these days; it must look well over a little silk frock at the cinema or for special dates; but it must also be practical for everyday hard wear.'*

Their solution was a coat *'made in one hundred per cent camel, gloriously soft and warm, in that creamy shade that is the true camel hair colour.'* Total cost – 6 guineas and eighteen coupons. Worthwhile, however, because: *'camel is very light to wear and exceedingly cosy, so it fulfils the first necessity of your winter coat. Also it will wear very much better and longer than the fancy weaves which used to be so smart for winter coats.'*

The style of the coat should be: *'collarless at the back, falling to wide revers at the front. It has a full-flared skirt, fluting round the hem and is belted tightly. Rows of double stitching round the edges form the only trimming and there are two deep, roomy pockets.'*

The recommended suit was quite expensive at $6\frac{1}{2}$ guineas but, as the article pointed out, it would have to last a long time. The material they suggested was a Harris tweed, brown or tan for city use, lighter or a check if you spent most of your time in the country. Again the style was simple, so as not to date; hip-length jacket with high revers and long buttoning, with three plain pockets

A four-year plan for a woman's wardrobe, from **Sew & Save**

First year
1 pair shoes
6 pairs stockings
10oz wool or 2½ yds material
1 suit
2 slips
1 blouse (home made)

Second year
1 pair shoes
6 pairs stockings
8oz wool or 2yds material
1 silk dress
Underwear: Cami-knickers or vest and knickers
(2 or 3 pairs)
Corselette or brassiere and girdle (2 or 3 pairs)
6 handkerchiefs

Third year
2 pairs shoes
6 pairs stockings
4oz wool or 1yd material
1 jacket
2 cotton or silk frocks
2 slips
1 pair of corsets

Fourth year
1 pair shoes
6 pairs stockings
6oz wool or 1½ yds material
1 woollen housecoat or dressing gown
Underwear: Cami-knickers or vest and knickers
(2 or 3 pairs)
Corselette or brassiere and girdle (2 or 3 pairs)
6 handkerchiefs

The ideal companion for slacks

...st tweeds for the country

the only trimming. The skirt being straight, just below the knee, with single inverted centre pleats, held by an arrowhead. Besides the advantages of easy matching and hard wearing, the suit was low maintenance: *'A suit like this will only need cleaning and occasional steaming and pressing to keep it in perfect shape.'*

The two-piece suit became an important part of women's dress, giving as it did three variations: a suit, a skirt, and a jacket.

The Board of Trade monitored how people used their coupons. During the first year of rationing women spent 18 per cent of their coupons on underwear and 23 per cent on frocks and coats, jackets and skirts. The remaining 59 per cent went on a whole range of goods, especially stockings, footwear, corsets and nightwear. In the second year there was a slight reduction in the purchase of underwear and a corresponding increase on outer garments.

One answer to the inevitable lack of stockings was to wear slacks, scandalous before the war, yet increasingly fashionable as the war went on, with their suggestion of war work. A letter to **Woman** in October 1941 pointed out that: *'There has always been a lot of controversy about the subject of slacks for women, but now the question of whether girls at work should wear them in the office has arisen. Surely there need be no controversy in times such as these. The main argument against slacks is that women are the wrong shape for them, and look most unattractive in them. That seems to me to be the last argument that is justifiable today. It surely doesn't matter a pin what a girl looks like if she is wearing clothes that are serviceable, comfortable and durable. Slacks are all three, and they save coupons for stockings. Bother our hips!'*

The response was: *'We disagree with your remark – "It surely doesn't matter a pin what a girl looks like ..." It matters a great deal, whatever the job. Looking nice doesn't lessen efficiency. Have you ever thought what a regiment on parade would look like in carpet slippers and creased, unbrushed uniforms? Yet many women, as soon as they put on slacks, immediately let their whole appearance go. They seem to think that slacks must go with sloppiness.*

'We quite agree that they are an economy and a great convenience in these days. And on some jobs they are necessary. But if women would take as much trouble over their general appearance when they put on slacks as they do when they wear their newest and smartest frocks, then the controversy would die away.'

In fact, it was generally admitted that shortages, and especially rationing, had a beneficial effect on women's appearance: *'As far as women's clothes are concerned, the combined*

◄ A good range of hand-knitted sweaters from 1942, note that puffed sleeves remained fashionable throughout.

▼ Women's slacks were typically full, buttoning at the left-hand side, and were often worn with a jumper, as shown.

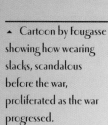

▲ Cartoon by Fougasse showing how wearing slacks, scandalous before the war, proliferated as the war progressed.

▸ A selection of women's coats from 1942. The short coat in the middle was typical of the period, and shows utility styling

effect of high-quality design for utility clothes and an enforced austerity in clothes of all kinds has been astonishingly good. The average woman's clothes may not be of as good material as they were in pre-war days and, as has already been stated, her shoes and stockings are certainly very much inferior, but the total impression which she makes is neater, often smarter, usually altogether more chic. Forced to do without frills, she has learned something of the French woman's appreciation of cut and line; limited by rationing to something less than half of her pre-war purchases, she has learned that colour, to be used with effect, must also be used with discretion and that the casual buying of clothes that happen to catch the eye is anything but a safeguard against the risk of having "nothing to wear".' **Civilian Supplies in Wartime Britain**.

In spite of all the problems there were still half-hearted attempts to create identifiable trends, **Woman and Home** declared, in February 1942: *'Solid top, patterned skirt – that's the theme of the new spring clothes.'* By this time, most of the advice was more practical in nature, faced with the realities of austerity and rationing:

'Just a word about clothes. Because it's winter, it doesn't mean you must only wear your darkest, drabbest clothes. I know they're more practical but just now and again when you want to look pretty give yourself a splash of colour, a gay set of collar and cuffs – bright blue mittens, a new coloured ribbon for your old felt hat. Tiny little things like these make a world of difference and help enormously to make you look fair and lovely in the snappiest cold snap.' **Home Companion**, November 1943.

By December 1944, **Woman** magazine, like many of its readers, was looking firmly ahead

to the post-war era, advising its readers in the Women's Forces: *'When you get back into civvies again, you will find that in the Services you learned a whole lot about dress, which is going to stand you in good stead.*

'Having learned how well a smart, simple suit can look, how important good grooming is, how comfortable and sensible low-heeled shoes are, how much it pays to have all the details right and simple, too, you'll keep that knowledge tucked inside your pretty heads and will not be led away by the effects of screen-glamour.

'Missing buttons, untied shoe-laces, press-studs that don't fasten, safety pins instead of stitches, seated skirts, wrinkled jackets, untidy hair, dirty shoes, missing gloves. It makes quite a list when you add it up. And if the girl from the Services is never guilty of any of these when she gets home, the other girls will have to look to their laurels.'

Teenagers, as such, were, by the beginning of the war, just beginning to emerge as a separate fashion group, rather than a sort of chrysalis-stage on the road to becoming a woman and women's magazines often had fashion tips for them: *'Take a tip from us – choose clothes that are simple and casual and gay – and see to it that they, and you, are always fresh as daisies. Try the new American vogue for wearing knee-tall socks in the country, with a short swing skirt and pageboy jacket. You'll be devastating!'* **Woman & Beauty**, November 1939.

'Her clothes must be simple – fussy suits and frocks will spoil the lines of her pretty young figure – "amusing" hats will give her an older sophistication and spoil her dewy freshness. Colours must count with her a lot ... there are so many youthful, happy shades that she may wear.

THEY WILL BE ON DUTY

From Now Until Spring

VIEW A.

VIEW B.

VIEW C.

Gone are the days when, with the first fall of leaves, you made a tweed coat, knowing that you could have a fur-trimmed one later on. Now the problem is whether you can spare the coupons for even one all-purpose coat to see you right through to Spring.

If you have decided that a new coat is essential you could not find a wiser investment for your coupons than our Special Pattern-of-the-Month. All three versions have the same easy-to-wear lines, shoulders well squared for comfort over a suit, and neckline so snug that you won't miss a fur collar. Take your choice of the belted town-coat, the brief, boxy jacket or the casual check tweed.

View A. 2½ or 2⅝ yards of 54-inch material.
View B. 2 yards of 54-inch material.
View C. 2½ or 2⅝ yards of 54-inch material.
(All for 36-inch bust measurements.)

BESTWAY
SPECIAL
PATTERN
No. 20,042
Price 1/6d.
By Post 1/7d.
Overseas 2/-.

This
Month's
THREE-FROM-ONE
SPECIAL
PATTERN

We always buy our clothes at Harrods "Junior Miss & 'teen-age Shop"

Bolero Suits . . .
Superbly tailored in a light weight woollen material with a simplicity of line that is always in good taste. In Navy, Brown or Black. Sizes 35-38 Hips.
£14 . 17 . 5 each.
(¾ length sleeve - 11 coupons).
(Short sleeve - 9 coupons).

HARRODS

'Let her take a leaf from Nature's lore – choose a suit of brightest moss green, wear with it a blouse of palest yellow, and so for all the world look like a daffodil. Let her wear the powdery blue of the first Scylla – what prettier outfit could she choose than a suit of pearly-grey worn with scylla blue accessories? Navy is practical, we know, and specially becoming to blue and grey eyes, but navy all alone is a sad story. Give almost any navy woollen frock collar and cuffs in dainty hyacinth pink, and see the difference! Wear primrose yellow with nutty brown, and if you want to look your prettiest avoid all hard colours such as bright reds and oranges, cyclamens, and harsh purples.

'Remember that for you a simply-cut suit or frock with a clever colour contrast in accessories is going to score all along the line.' **Lady's Companion**, February 1940.

Of course, austerity, shortages and clothes rationing held back any further development of teenage fashions for a few more years.

Special maternity clothes could be bought, but worn as they were for such a short time, they really weren't 'coupon-value'. It was far more common to pass them round, or to convert existing clothes, as this advice from the **Home Companion** of September 1943 shows: *You can easily make a most suitable affair from an old summer frock. Cut the top off the dress at the yoke, leave out the rest of the bodice and the yoke altogether, then join the full gathered skirt straight on to the yoke!'*

Or using a pre-war ball gown: *'Dyed a darker colour there's enough stuff here to make you a really useful frock. The newest "before baby" ones have the fullness of the bodice and waist gathered into dainty ribbon drawstrings – such a clever way of keeping a secret this and a really young and clever style.*

'An odd scrap of lace frilled into the neck will keep your little frock looking fresh and cool on summer days, or you could give interest to the frock by having the ribbon tie-ups in a darker shade.'

Most older, working-class women wore a dress under an apron ('pinny'), often with a headscarf, with an overcoat and shopping bag for outdoor wear. The middle-class, having more money, and often more time, tended to remain more fashion conscious as they grew older. The magazines were full of advice for them, too:

'Panelled skirts and slightly bloused bodices do much to minimize the older woman's figure, and slightly squared shoulders help too. She should wear sleeves that fit at the wrists.

'Wide belts, fussy skirts and fitting bodices emphasise a spreading figure, so beware of them. And remember that Raglan shoulders are not always very becoming.' **Woman's Weekly**, December 1939.

The item of clothing which best conjures up the early part of the war was the shelter

◄ Teenage fashions from 1945. The teenager would not become a truly separate fashion entity for another decade.

▼ A range of fashions for 'Young looking bigger sizes', a euphemism for the middle-aged, from late 1942.

suit, now known as the siren suit. At first it was a practical solution to being woken in the middle of the night by the warning, and having to rush to the shelter, because the wearer could dress warmly and quickly. The all-in-one shelter suit was the practical solution to this problem, but it soon became a fashion item for those better-off women who wanted to look patriotic, as this excerpt from **William Does his Bit** demonstrates:

"'Gosh," said William excitedly. "I can hear bombs."
'But it was only the Bevertons arriving.
'Mrs Beverton was inordinately stout and her daughter was inordinately thin. They were both dressed in the latest siren suits, and had obviously taken great pains with their make-up and coiffeurs. Mrs Beverton wore a three-stringed pearl necklace, large jade earrings and four bracelets. She had, moreover, used a new exotic perfume that made William cry out in genuine alarm "Gas! Where's my gas mask?"'

Other such items of predominantly middle- and upper-class wartime dress were the tin helmet, (worn with pearls by upper-class girls driving ambulances), usually accompanied by slacks. These later gave way to uniforms, for those in the women's auxiliary services and an ever-expanding group of civilian services, such as the ARP, the WVS, the Land Army and the Red Cross. Many women who joined the auxiliary forces – the Auxiliary Territorial Service, Women's Auxiliary Air Force, the Women's Royal Naval Service – chose to do so on the basis of which uniform they preferred: the khaki of the ATS, the grey-blue of the WAAFs or the dark blue of the WRNS. The rigours of their wartime duties meant that many women were far fitter and muscular than they had been pre-war, often with the result was that when they went home on leave, they found that their old civilian clothes no longer fitted.

As the war went on, it became a must for older women in the higher social orders to be seen in clothes which emphasised 'make do and mend' or suggested that their wearer was too deeply involved in war-work to bother about their clothes. By 1944, Kathleen

▸ Siren suits, or as they were more popularly known, shelter suits. Note the gas mask bags.

Wallace, writing in **Good Housekeeping** commented: *'I wonder, not for the first time, why your true British matron must wear hand-knitted woollen jumpers when she is a solid 44 (measurement, please, not age), why she effects a beret, a form of head-gear which I, personally, feel only becomes the troops, and the younger troops at that.'*

For increasing numbers of women the factory became their workplace, affecting their everyday dress, as described in the book, **Munition Girl**: *'The Industrial Army has no recognised uniform, like that of the Services, but this does not mean that the clothing of the munitions girl is unimportant. Far from it ...*

'You will feel better, will work better, and on some dangerous jobs will last longer, if you are dressed for the part. Clothing will, of course, depend on the type of work, and should afford ease of movement and protection from any particular dangers connected with the job.

'It is essential that suitable headgear should be worn in certain processes. ... A cap must completely cover the hair, as stray curls, or even wisps of hair, can be caught up in a machine and result in partial scalping. ... Turbans, which are fashionable and generally accepted by employers and in Government Training Centres, are a popular form of head protection. Another design of headgear perhaps meets all requirements. It is a net cap which can be put on without upsetting hairstyles; the peak affords protection against straying curls and the net will hold a roll or long hair at the back. An adjustable strip of material going round the head holds the cap firmly in place.

'Overalls can be of many types and designs, but they should be close fitting and comfortable and easy to launder. The ordinary coat-type is generally worn, but zip fastenings are effective, and stand more strain than buttons. Back or shoulder fastening overalls, whether of the tunic or trousered type, are somewhat safer than those buttoned at the front. Short sleeves are preferable when working on or near machines, and long sleeves should be close fitting at the wrist or, better still, be rolled up above the elbows.'

Not everyone took such advice. Mass Observation recorded: *'In the same carefree spirit, [Peggy] always wears nice dresses and stockings to work, regardless of the fact that among the dirt and oil* of the machine shop they are going to be ruined very quickly. Asked how she will manage about coupons, she says gaily:

'"Oh, I don't know, I expect my brother will give me some. I'm not going to come in slops for anybody. I've always worn nice things to work, and they aren't going to stop me."'

'Molly – "It's so difficult. I can't decide what to do for the summer, I want to save my cotton dresses. I don't want to wear them for work, they'll get filthy. Are those slacks very hot? I did think of those – I think they're all right if you're on war work don't you? I don't think they're very nice for girls in the ordinary way. Or I might buy a skirt, and wear one of those dark shirt blouses with it.

'It's terrible the way the dirt gets through on to your clothes. I was ashamed of my petticoat this week, it was all quite black."' from **War Factory** – a report by Mass Observation. For most women, work clothes were represented by one item – the pinafore or 'pinny'. An apron, 'with or without bib' used up three coupons, yet make do and mend, and of course the hus- band's clothes, were there to help: *When she's stumped for a pinny to wear about the house she begs old shirts from hubby, because they make beauties. She takes off the collar band, neatens the neck, shortens the sleeves and makes a waistband from the cut off tail part and there it is. She wears it back to front because it then looks for all the world like a country smock!'* **Home Companion,** July 1943. **Sew & Save** recommended: *'Never throw away faded or torn cotton frocks, and rather than tear them up for dusters, make yourself house-aprons with them. You can get two aprons from every frock. Cut out the sleeves, then from the lower arm-hole cut straight across the top. The side-seams should be cut open, then hemmed down flat again. The back and front bodices are hemmed into square bibs. A couple of yards of rib- bon, or coloured tape to attach to the bib of*

each apron, taken back over the shoulders, crossed over at the back, and brought round to tie at the waist-front will complete the garment.'

There were other tricks to cope with messy jobs, too. A pair of old stockings could still see service. With the feet cut off they made excellent arm protectors for dirty jobs such as flue cleaning, or awkward jobs such as fruit picking.

With the outbreak of war and the sudden call-up of men to the Forces, many were in a rush to get married. In 1939 marriages

◄ Woman's bib-and-brace overalls. An increasing number of women were conscripted into industry as the war progressed.

▼ Pinnies: an advert from the Ministry of Fuel and Power which shows how the pinafore was the uniform for housewives of all ages.

increased by 21 per cent on 1938. This often meant foregoing a full traditional white wedding. But weddings soon settled to a more traditional look, although the two-piece suit, decorated with an elaborate corsage, remained a popular and practical option throughout the war. The main difference in early wartime weddings was that many of those present, including the groom, would be in uniform.

The advent of rationing changed wartime weddings dramatically. A whole year's supply of coupons would not provide all an 'old-fashioned' bride would need. With just enough coupons to keep you decent, who was going to use them on a dress you would only wear once? Many wartime brides opted for a smart suit which could be re-used for special occasions.

Some did still try to have a white wedding. Hire shops did a good trade, and previously used dresses were taken out of moth-balls and did the rounds of family and friends. Patricia McGuire remembers one wedding in 1942: *'The Bride had a white dress, more grey looking than white, as it had been used so many times before'*.

You could always make it yourself but even that would require many coupons for the amount of material in the traditional wedding dress. Parachute silk was just the job (if you could get it) and some even used the light green silk retrieved from German land-mine parachutes. But for many the answer was a borrowed white dress and a veil made up from net. Few home-made wedding dresses of the period remain today as the material would soon be reused for other things.

For most, some attempt at a new outfit for the bride, groom, and bridesmaids was attempted, but for the guests, this was largely impossible. For most guests a wedding outfit meant a new hat. The **Home Companion** of April 1943 advised: *'camouflaging the mooring elastic of your everyday hat with a garland of flowers'* for use at a wedding; or: *'If you want a saucy hat to go to a late summer wedding in, how about*

this? Use a coffee saucer to cut a neat little circle of felt from an old black hat. Now cover the circle with black net, frill black or silk lace over it rosette fashion, and perch a big, frivolous pink rose in the centre. Perch your little hat over your curls, tie it on with pink ribbons tying in a bow at the back and there you are.'

Underwear comprised of knickers, either 'directoire' knickers, often called bloomers, which were long drawers with elastic at the end of the legs, or 'French' knickers, like boxer shorts. Directoire knickers had been part of popular fashion since the First World War, as they were a necessity with the fashion for short skirts. French knickers were regarded as old fashioned as they were potentially revealing under shorter skirts. All that changed with rubber shortages, which meant elastic was difficult to obtain. French knickers, fastened by buttons at the side, used very little elastic, and were therefore only two coupons whereas directoires required three.

Rationing also brought in an unexpected problem for the women of the Forces. *'Men and girls joining the Services will have to surrender their clothing coupons to a responsible military, naval or air force authority'*, while those already in the Forces were not issued with a ration book. This would not seem at first glance to be a problem – they were issued with uniform – but many women found the issue underwear pretty awful; they were commonly called passion-killers.

▼ A range of women's nightwear and underwear from 1941.

"you might knit or tat a brassiere from crochet cotton"

However, underwear was an area ripe for make do and mend. For those not brilliant at needlework it was ideal, as the finished results were not on public display. The same applied to the materials involved; a wide range of fabrics could be used, and you could save coupons for garments which were more difficult to make.

By the 1940s, the bra was worn either separately, or as part of a corselette, a full-length corset. For those with smaller busts, brassieres were much more flimsy.

'Here is an idea for making very dainty brassieres for small figures from a prettily trimmed handkerchief. Fold the handkerchief diagonally in halves and cut along the fold. Fold each of the resulting triangles in halves, with the fold running from apex to centre base. Mark the darts thus: along the raw edge (from the crease) measure 1 in. and along the crease measure 2 ins. Connect these points for the dart. Overlap the two triangles at their base for 2 ins., stitch the dart with a run and fell seam, and join ribbon straps to the apexes of the triangles for shoulder straps. Take a length of ribbon measuring half the bust plus 2 ins., neaten both ends and fold in halves. Insert the raw edge of the brassiere in between the ribbon and stitch strongl., Sew a length of ribbon to each end to tie at the back. Pass the shoulder straps over the shoulder and make a loop at the ends for the waist straps to pass through.' **The Pictorial Guide to Modern Home Dressmaking**, 1940.

Alternatively you might knit or tat a brassiere from crochet cotton, darted over the diaphragm and supported across the back with wide elastic.

Not everyone wore a brassiere. For many, especially working-class girls, underwear consisted of drawers, with cotton interlock

vest, or combinations, or perhaps a liberty corselette, a sort of combination liberty bodice and suspenders.

While stockings were still available, they were held up by suspenders, either on a belt, or incorporated into a corset, full-length corselette, liberty bodice or the elastic roll-on 'ideal for wear under dance-frocks and for sports'. You might also knit your own suspenders in crochet cotton and fix the slides and ends of worn-out suspenders on to them. Or, until elastic itself became scarce, you could make your own belt with suspenders bought from the haberdashery counter

(opposite)
Cami-knickers.

▼ Bottom right –
directoire knickers
were popular at the
start of the war, but
needed more
coupons than
French knickers.

"MUST-HAVES" for the NOT-SO-SLIM

All the designs on this page are modelled in 36, 38, 40, 44 and 48-inch bust sizes, also in a special short length size with a 44-inch bust measurement.

(Right) You do need a cardigan but with so much knitting for the men in the Forces you have no time to knit for yourself. The solution, then, is to copy No. 19,992 in wool stockinette. You'll find it simple to make and very well-shaped.
For the 40-inch bust size allow 1⅛ yards of 54-inch material.

Bestway Pattern No. 19,992
Price 1/3d.
By Post 1/4d.
Overseas 2/-

Bestway Pattern No. 19,996
Price 1/6d.
By Post 1/7d.
Overseas 2/-

Bestway Pattern No. 19,994
Price 1/6d.
By Post 1/7d.
Overseas 2/-

Bestway Pattern No. 19,964
Price 1/3d.
By Post 1/4d.
Overseas 2/-

For your leisure moments, you will want a graceful frock to slip into so we suggest No. 19,996 copied in a dark ground printed silk. Although it is cut to take a minimum of material, you will find its soft bodice and panelled skirt very figure-flattering.
For the 40-inch bust size allow 3¼ or 3⅜ yards of 36-inch material.

If you are an out-of-uniform war-worker, you need a frock that will help to keep you smart and efficient-looking throughout the busiest day, and No. 19,994 with its neat tailored lines and absence of fussy details, fits the bill perfectly.
For the 40-inch bust size allow 2¼ or 2⅜ yards of 54-inch material.

(Right) For the woman who has difficulty in buying lingerie that really fits, the knicker pattern No. 19,964 will be a boon. Darts at waist and knee ensure a smooth line, with ample room for movement.
For the 48-inch hip size, allow 1⅜ yards of 36-inch or 1⅛ yards of 54-inch material.

stitched onto a belt made of wide elastic.

Over all this went a petticoat, underslip or underskirt. An alternative was cami-knickers, combining a camisole and knickers, which fastened under the crotch. You could turn a slip into cami-knickers fairly easily by short-ening it to the right length and making a gusset from the left over bits. The gusset was then stitched on 3 inches above the hem at the back, and fixed with press-studs on to the front of the garment.

One of the things which seems very strange to us nowadays is the fact that people had far fewer sets of underwear then, even before rationing, and often wore them for much longer than we would think hygienic. *You know that no American girl would ever dream of wearing the same pair of stockings two days run-ning. Few of them wear the same undies two days running either. They run them through with water every night before going to bed, and I can't help wondering whether the lovely clean feeling that this is bound to give them underneath may not be respon-sible for their amazing band-box looks. If you've got the kind of undies that don't need ironing this is very easy to do, and a trick worth two if you're one of the unfortunate ones who perspire very freely during the warm weather.'* **Home Companion.**

In the 1943 film **Millions Like Us** about conscripted factory girls, one upper-class girl is appalled when her new working-class room-mate gets into bed in her underwear.

'You're not getting into bed like that?'

'Like what?'

'Without undressing.'

'But I have undressed.'

'Aren't you going to take your underclothes off?'

'Why? They've only got to go on again in the morning. You are fussy!'

And not just underwear. The book, **Keep Fit in Wartime** by Dr Harry Roberts lays down a dozen rules of health, including number eight: *'Cultivate bodily cleanliness. Wash the entire surface of the body every morning and every evening; and, so far as practicable, brush the teeth after every meal. Don't pay so much attention to what the outside of your clothes looks like, as to the state of your skin and your underwear. At the same time it is a good plan to brush or beat all your clothes every day; the dust may easily harbour the germs of all sorts of diseases.'* **The Home Companion**, of July 1943, pointed out: *'No matter what your job your feet need washing at least once a day'.*

In many ways life was very different from today. Hot water was not on tap in the way we expect and showers were unusual in domestic settings. As in peacetime, people tended to bathe about once every week to ten days. They were also urged to save fuel by only filling the bath to a depth of 5 inches. Although deodorant existed, women wore it far more than men. Generally people were far more relaxed about smelling a little sweaty than is the case today.

Only the most expensive of modern flats would have had central heating, and as double glazing was non-existent, houses were often cold and draughty. Moreover, many people could not afford nightwear, so stripping off only the top layers of clothes was the perfect answer. For those who did run to nightwear, the nightdress was common. Only among the younger, smarter set did women wear pyjamas, although their use increased with the war, and the need to go down to the shelter at night.

CHILDREN

'Plus-fours would make two pairs of shorts for a school-boy. Pyjama legs will make children's vests. Woollen stockings with worn feet can have the legs opened down the back seams and can then be made up into an infant's jersey.' Make Do and Mend

The items that make up a baby's wardrobe, or layette, have not greatly changed since the nineteen-forties, although the materials used have undergone huge changes, with forties babies' clothing made of such wonderfully-named materials as nun's veiling and delaine (both woollen material), nainsook (fine soft cotton), and piqué (a stiff, ribbed cotton).

Pilches, or pilch knickers, had short elasticated legs, while being full enough to go over a nappy.

Petticoats were made from very fine flannel, or from nainsook, cambric or fine cotton. Matinee jackets might be of corded silk, piqué, muslin, crepe-de-chine, or fine flannel for winter wear. Binders would be made from soft white cotton flannel, and vests knitted in silk and wool. Frocks and night-gowns of warm woolly material such as loosely woven flannel or Viyella. Other materials used were fine muslin and lace or embroidery for the wrists, necks and hems.

When rationing was first introduced, babies' clothing did not need coupons, but coupons were required for the material or wool used to hand-make clothes. Soon babies' clothing was brought into the rationing scheme and, just two months after the scheme had begun, clothing ration cards for babies were issued. Every expectant mother, as soon as her pregnancy was confirmed by her doctor, was entitled to receive fifty clothing coupons (in the case of twins an extra fifty would be issued at birth, or upon definite diagnosis). These came in units of five and could not be divided, so it was important to plan out the babies layette well in advance. At birth, further coupons would be issued, depending on the date of birth (in the rationing calendar), from a minimum of ten, up to a maximum of forty.

A TYPICAL BABY'S LAYETTE

4 DAY GOWNS

3 FLANNEL BINDERS

3 SILK AND WOOL VESTS

3 LONG SOFT WOOL OR FINE FLANNEL PETTICOATS

4 NIGHTDRESSES (FINE COTTON OR CAMBRIC)

6 BIBS

2 WOOLLEN BONNETS

2 WOOL COATEES, OR MATINEE JACKETS

3 PAIRS WOOLLEN BOOTEES

4 PILCHES

2 DOZ. GAUZE SQUARES

2 DOZ. SQUARES OF TERRY TOWELLING

1 WOOLLEN SHAWL

3 PAIRS GLOVES

▼ A 'buster' suit.

▸ Evacuee boys' 'Home
Guard'. A good selection
of boys' clothes and haircuts; note the child's tin
helmet. (Crown Copyright)

Suggested wardrobe for a baby under rationing, **Mother and Home** magazine, February 1942:

TO BUY	READY MADE
4 vests	4 coupons
3 over-all leggings	6 coupons
3 petticoats	6 "
3 flannel bodices	3 "
3 frocks	9 "
3 flannel pilches	1 "
4 nightgowns	12 "
3 pairs knickers	3 "
3 coatees	3 "
pram coat	5 "
3 pairs bootees	1 "
3 bibs	1 "
large shawl	4 "
soft napkins	coupon free
small shawl	2 "
Turkish towelling napkins	1 coupon each
3 jerseys	6 "
handkerchiefs	1 coupon for 4

Mother and Home went on to show how many of the above could be hand-knitted or made up, thereby saving coupons because although wool and material both needed coupons, in making them you needed fewer coupons than the same garments bought ready-made.

The following are descriptions of the sort of clothes worn by children whose families could afford to keep up with the latest fashions in children's wear. For the less well-off, hand-me-downs had always been the fashion, but most would wear similar clothes to the ones described.

When they moved on from baby clothes, children would wear, for outside use, a pram set: a coat and bonnet, often with leggings for colder weather, all made from wool, Rayon, corduroy, or similar. Indoors, for either sex, a frock or romper suit was the fashion; both frock or rompers would probably be of cotton, with embroidery or smocking across the chest. Romper suits were very similar to dresses but with two elasticated leg holes, and both were fastened at the back of the neck.

Next came the toddlers. Leggings, or a footless version, legginettes, looking rather like long spats, were the fashion for outdoor use, with a legging – or legginette-suit used for best. For indoors, bib-and-brace sets were popular, or for boys, jersey suits, comprising of knitted shirt and shorts (more commonly called 'knickers'), or similar 'buster' suits, comprising a short-sleeved shirt and shorts made from art silk or cotton. The two were made of different, often contrasting, colours, with the shirt collar, and often a sleeve edging, in the same colour as the shorts. The two parts were buttoned together. For girls, short dresses were the thing, in cotton for everyday, or art silk or velvet for best. This would be the same for most children, only the quality of the material used would change according to the family's means.

For older children, aged up to about six or seven, both girls and boys, dungarees were a popular garment to substitute when the romper stage was over. Woollen jersey shirts or shirt blouses were usually worn underneath.

Both boys and girls wore similar under-wear, pilch knickers, and short sleeved vests, and for girls, simple petticoats, often with matching pilch knickers, would go with frocks.

Footwear for the youngest was made of fabric, or soft leather. Once walking, the most popular shoes for both boys and girls were sandals, with ankle bars for the younger children and some girls, but more commonly, t-bars for both sexes. Some boys wore lace-up shoes, or even boots for rough wear. Early in the war, wellingtons and plimsolls were a common sight, (Liverpool was nicknamed 'plimsoll city' from their preponderance among its evacuees), but as the war went on, shortage of rubber meant they became a rarity.

Under rationing, children's clothing was rated at a lower coupon-value than similar articles for adult use, and children received extra coupons. This was meant to compensate for children's extra needs but it also meant that children's clothes were a good alternative for smaller adults.

▾ A typical knitted shirt, worn by both boys and girls. It was quite common to see such shirts worn with a school tie knotted over the top, as with an ordinary shirt.

Special allowances for older children and for those growing abnormally quickly were introduced and were modified from time to time. In spite of this many mothers felt the allowances were insufficient; children, then as now, got through clothes at an alarming rate.

It was far more common to make clothes for children than for adults, and women's magazines, especially those designed for working-class women, such as **Woman's Weekly** or the **Home Companion**, had always

been full of patterns to make or knit children's clothes. And the younger the child, the more common it was to make the clothes.

The book, **War Time Needlework,** told its readers that: *'Delightful summer frocks can be made for the four to five year-old girl from a shirt that has a blue and white or pink and white stripe. Darker stripes look rather too heavy on a young child, but a little frock in pastel stripes and bound with rick-rack braid, or with cherry-coloured or royal blue tape, is charming. If you are cutting down clothes for a younger child from those of an older one, or cutting down from your own or your husband's clothes, do have the patience to unpick the garment and entirely re-make it for the child. Children do so love to have something new that is completely their own, and it is really hardly any more trouble to remake for a child than to take in and fit and re-fit the same model so that it comes out looking just the same only a size smaller.'*

Once again, men's wardrobes provided the raw materials: *'From a man's discarded shirt enough sound material can be salvaged to make a school blouse for a small girl. Father's old flannel trousers provide stuff for a warm little frock; use the top part for the bodice and make a gored skirt from the leg portions. Trim with contrasting collar and cuffs.'* Board of Trade, April 1943.

As the war went on, more ingenuity was needed to recycle material: *'Suppose you're making a frock out for your wee girl out of a remnant of material. You pin your pattern pieces hopefully to it, but juggle as you may you find it can't be done. You're short of material, you're stumped, and what do you do? If you're wise you cut out the skirt and the bodice, then collect the remnants, patchwork them neatly together on the machine, then cut sleeves and collar from the big patched piece. If the material is patterned you'll have to go carefully and match up the design, but no matter if the job is tricky, you get there in the end, and that bonny little frock becomes yet another flag for victory.'* **Home Companion,** August 1943.

Another idea was a frock for a two year-old made from an adult's machine-knitted jumper. These, you were assured, would not run when cut if you turned in the seams and

bound them at once. You could also use knitwear which had gone 'felty' to make mittens for the older children, pixie caps for windy days, and in-soles for their bedroom slippers. If the wool had become a dingy-looking off-white, the advice was to dip the new garment in cold coffee.

Other advice aimed to keep clothes going longer by cutting down on wear and tear: *'When my little boy was at the crawling stage, the worn-out toes of his shoes were my despair until I thought of a way of preserving them. I cut two half cir-cles out of an old pair of gloves and stitched round the curved edge, making a pocket to fit the toe of the shoe. A piece of tape stitched to each side tied round baby's ankle. I embroidered a small flower on the front of each to make them pretty. Any soft leather or felt could be used.'* Reader's letter to **Mother** magazine, May 1944.

Better still was to make clothes with future patching in mind: *'It is a wise plan when making children's jumpers and jerseys to knit a square about 2½ inches in the same pattern as the body and stitch into the elbow of each sleeve. This greatly prolongs the life of the garment.'* **My Weekly,** March 1940.

'When you are making summer frocks for a little girl, always sew an odd piece of material into the waist of the frock so that it gets washed every time the frock is washed, and provides a piece of material for patching the same colour as the frock itself. Even the fastest of fast colours seem to wilt when worn by children.' **Sew & Save**.

From the ages of six to fourteen, children's clothes went slowly through a transition into adult clothing. There was only the faintest inkling at this time of a separate fashion group in the early teenage years.

Sew & Save described the schoolgirl's wardrobe: *'The most important item in her wardrobe is, of course, her school uniform, usually a gym-slip and blouse. Usually, schools like children to wear knickers to match the slip, and even if there is no rule about this it is a good economy measure. A gym-slip and knickers to match take 2⅛ yards of 54-inch material for a little girl 7-8 years old, while 2⅞ yards are needed for a 14 year-old.'* Ties were common

Utility overcoat for a girl. Notice also the t-bar sandals and the hair style. (Crown Copyright)

for both boys' and girls' school uniforms, the most common being machine knitted, with inch-wide horizontal stripes in school colours. Hats were part of the uniform, often felt or straw, brimmed hats with a wide band in the school colours, or berets, on which the school badge or monogram was sewn. For younger girls the beret, or the pixie hood were favourite. They commonly wore long woollen stockings, usually black, blue or brown, and only the oldest girls wore real stockings.

Outside school, girls would wear a simple dress, or skirt with blouse or jumper. For girls up to eleven or twelve, dungarees still might be worn. With the outbreak of war the shelter or siren suit became popular, but dungarees made a come-back with Dig for Victory, having become popular items of uniform in the Women's Land Army. Older girls would wear dresses rather like smaller versions of their mother's.

Boys' uniform typically comprised of a blazer, cap, short trousers worn with long woollen socks up to the age of twelve or thirteen, then long trousers. Clothes were made to last: *'For winter, serge, face-cloth, rep, and branded woollens made specially in narrow widths for children's wear are the best choice. For summer, choose fabrics that will wash well and easily, like rayon, cotton, muslin, lawn and voile.'* Although they were bought or made with lots of 'growing room', even so they often began to show signs of wear and tear. It is surprising how much extra wear can be got out of children's clothes by reinforcement at the right places. For example: *'"Anchorage" or buttons. A sudden tug often brings away a button and a bit of material too. This is less likely to happen if you back each button with a small circle of material on the wrong side of the garment, and sew well through,'* advised the Board of Trade. And: *'If a boy's jacket is badly worn at the elbows, patches from a worn out pair of leather gloves will save the day. The patches should be in the form of a semi-circle, sewn in with the straight line to the outer sleeve seam and the rounded edge stitched down towards the inside of the elbow.'*

Even with growing room thrown in, clothes soon became too small. The **Home Companion**

▸ A selection of girls' fashions from 1944.

ppy Holiday Frocks

CHILDREN still get holidays—and don't they love a change from school clothes! The four charming frock patterns shown here will please mothers, too—for they can be used for making new frocks for young daughters, or renovating old ones—as you see, combining plain and patterned materials.

Patterns cost 1/- each up to 10 years, 1/3d. each over, plus 1d. postage in every case, from " Home Notes," The Pattern Shop, Tower House, Southampton Street, London, W.C.2

Frock
61 A & B
years

Frock
67 A & B
years

(Left) Frock
No. 11,663 A & B
8-16 years

(Right) Frock
No. 11,662 A & B
6-12 years

suggested: *'When you knit her jumpers, start from the shoulders and work down. Make the ribbed welt at the waist detachable, and when she grows it will be an easy matter to unpick it, and lengthen the jumpers a couple of inches before you sew the welt on again.'*

Much could be knitted; jumpers, sweaters and cardigans, of course, but knitting books of the period also give patterns for socks, stockings, girls' hats, balaclavas, scarves, gloves, hair bows, underwear, and, even the dreaded knitted swimming costume!

Girls' dresses, blouses, coats and under-

◄ Typical young boy's outfit. Notice the shorts which were far tighter in the leg than is often assumed. Notice also, from the waist up, that the outfit is virtually the same as the man's outfit on page 3.

▲ Boy's zip-fronted knitted wind-jammer from 1940.

wear could all be hand-made, but you were not advised to make coats or trousers for older boys. Younger boys, however, were a different matter: *'Ever thought about making Sonny a neat little wind-proof jerkin from Daddy's old raincoat? He'll feel a real little tough in one that has a knitted welt at wrists and waist and this cosy ribbing will keep out the draught ... Make it battle-dress-style, and if you stitch a sergeant's stripes on the sleeve, and a row of "medal ribbons" across the pocket your cut-me-down will rejoice any boy's heart so that he'd be pleased as punch to wear it.'* The **Home Companion**.

Strangely enough, even at the height of clothes rationing, the government made no attempt to limit schools' demands for school uniform. Thus some of the more rigid institutions continued to demand full uniforms which needed more than a child's annual allocation of coupons. For most children their school uniform had to serve as their 'best' clothes for church, social events, etc.

This, and the everyday problems of hard-wear and growing meant that clothing children was a particular problem. In September 1941 a schoolmaster from Ewell had the idea of setting up a scheme to exchange children's clothes among his pupils' parents, and asked the local WVS to help. The success of this 'clothing exchange' led to several others being set up and the Board of Trade asked the WVS to operate the scheme nationally.

Collections of second-hand clothing were made to provide the initial stock for exchange; these collections became progressively more difficult because, post-rationing, few people had any old clothes to give away, so a make do and mend party was attached to almost every clothing exchange to convert depressing rejects into attractive garments.

The scheme worked on a points system. You took in one or more items of clean clothing that your child had grown out of, these would be assessed and points given to you depending on the item of clothing – similar to rationing – and its condition. You could then 'spend' the points on items of clothing in store at the exchange, each of which had been similarly assessed. At first both clothing and shoes were handled together at the same exchanges, but this led to shortages as clothes were exchanged for harder-to-get shoes; it was therefore decided that, in larger centres, separate shoe-exchanges should be set up. The scheme for shoes worked on the same principles as that for clothing, each pair of shoes brought in being assessed – five points for good as new, three for slightly worn, and one for shoes badly needing repair.

Within a few months the WVS were running 383 clothing exchanges plus nine mobile exchanges serving remote areas. What had been common practice among poorer families – mending, converting, and handing-down clothes between friends and family –

was now widely accepted, not only as a necessity, but as a patriotic duty.

In May 1944, a writer in **Mother** magazine commented: *'Five years ago the thought would have appalled me, and if I had mentioned it at all it would have been in whispers, but yesterday, Elizabeth came cycling up behind me in the village street and shouting at the top of her voice:*

"'Just coming round to tell you! Robin has grown out of his size eights and they're ready for your Gillian. And by the way, I've got that maternity corset for you. Jan sent it back this morning. Now she's scouring the countryside for an elastic girdle, but I told her I'd bagged yours for myself. Sure you won't want it back after-wards? They're as rare as gold."

'Yes, we talk like that. We live like that. We wear with pride and intense satisfaction those once-scorned things – cast-off clothes! And we don't pre-tend about it. Nor do we say any more, with a faint stammer and a bit of blushing: "I hope you won't be offended, Mrs. Brown, but I have some things of Anne's that would just fit your Joan. They're rather too good to throw away and I thought perhaps, if you don't mind taking them ..."

'We hail a woman like that with a hearty "Lead me to them!" Or we tackle her first "I have a pair of wellingtons that will fit Anne, and I'll swap with anything that will fit Joan – nighties if you have them."'

By the end of the war there were more than five hundred clothing and shoe exchanges across the country.

▸ Coventry, November 1940. Notice the two youths, dressed pretty much as their fathers might be. There was little in the way of teenage boys' fashion.

RATIONING
AUSTERITY & UTILITY

T he Board of Trade produced a series of 'Orders' which tightly controlled the way in which many items, including clothing, could be made. These were called 'austerity' provisions, and included such measures as the Cotton, Linen and Rayon Order, the Making of Civilian Clothing (Restrictions) Order, and the Limitation of Supplies (Cloth and Apparel) Order, to name but a few. Even official publications such as **Civilian Supplies in Wartime Britain** had to admit that: *'Some of these regulations are tiresome and a few are foolish. Taken together they tend, inevitably, to make for monotony in dress.'*

Austerity dictated how much clothing a manufacturer could produce, forbade the use of embroidery, limited the depth of hems and prohibited the use of certain materials. On men's clothing, regulations banned double-breasted jackets and turned-up trousers, while for both sexes they limited the amount of stitching and the number of buttons that might be used.

As early as September 13, 1939, the **Daily Mirror** was reporting that: *'Prices of all clothing, including underwear and footwear, are likely to rise as soon as stocks now held by retailers are cleared ... The [Men's Wear] Council advises the public to buy now, as even next January's sale prices may well be higher than those ruling today.'* The main reasons were shortages of raw materials due to the war, and an increasing shortage of labour as more men were called up.

" *You know, dear, if I were to cut off your turn-ups and sleeve buttons and sew up a few pockets I could make it look* JUST *like one of the fashionable Utility Suits.*"

▲ The utility suit.
Cartoon by Sillince.

Throughout the first eighteen months of the war, the amount of clothing for sale in the shops decreased, and prices increased. By April 1941, clothes prices had risen to 72 per cent above their 1939 level.

Clothes rationing was announced on June 1, 1941. The idea of rationing was not new to people; food had been rationed since January 1940. Then, people were informed well in advance; it had been announced on November 29, 1939. This forward notice had been a necessary part of the scheme, as consumers had to register with a retailer of each rationed item. This advance notice, however, had one obvious drawback.

Anyone with the will, and money, to do so, had plenty of time to hoard the items to be rationed. The government was determined that this would not be the case with clothes rationing and everything possible was done to keep it secret.

The two main problems which had required early notification were registration with retailers, and the printing and supply of ration books. The first did not apply to clothing as consumers were to be allowed to use clothing coupons in any shop. The second problem presented a bigger headache: printing millions of ration books would have been such a mammoth undertaking, that keeping it secret would have been impossible. The answer was to accept that it *was* impossible and to find an alternative. Everyone already had a food ration book, not every page of which was used; it included twenty-six unused margarine coupons. With the agreement of the Ministry of Food, it was decided to use them as clothing coupons.

Clothes rationing was now ready to be implemented. The Clothes Rationing Order was signed in secret on May 29, and announced on June 1, the day of its introduction. Being Whit Sunday, the public, and more urgently, retailers, had two days to prepare before the shops opened on Tuesday.

The rationing itself was stringent. Everybody over the age of four was to receive 66 coupons for the first year; these would just about be enough to buy one complete change of clothes. The 66 coupons were to be the twenty-six unused margarine coupons, to which would later be added another forty specially printed coupons on a green card.

Every item of clothing, including material and knitting wool, was covered by the scheme. Each garment was given a coupon value, reflecting the amount of materials and work involved. The customer could choose how to spend their coupons based on their own needs and tastes, and what was available. From the retailer's point of view, items could only be obtained from the wholesaler on production of coupons received from sales of current stocks.

It was by nature a complicated system, and the Board of Trade issued a half-page advert in that Sunday's papers setting out the basics of the scheme. The list of rationed items was huge, covering everything from everyday clothes to specialist items such as academic robes, vicars' surplices, and ballet shoes. The list of exceptions and special cases made life even more complicated. Second-hand clothes were exempt, but what exactly constituted second-hand clothing? What was to stop unscrupulous retailers selling new clothes as second-hand? Children's clothes needed fewer coupons, but what were children's clothes? Could a small adult buy children's clothes, and what of a large child who needed adult sizes? To try to answer some of these problems, the Board of Trade issued the **Clothing Coupon Quiz** in August. This included long lists of rationed goods and their coupon values, non-rationed goods, including 'apparel made of paper or feathers', as well as the answers to many common (and some uncommon) questions. Examples of the latter include: *'Can one buy a single shoe, sock, glove, or other article from a pair for half the number of coupons?' Answer: 'Yes, if the shopkeeper does not object.'*

Inevitably there was some complaining, especially from the better-off who would be worst hit, and from retailers whose trade would be badly affected. But there was a general acceptance that the war required belt-tightening and what better way than a system of fair shares for all? There was considerable counter-complaining about feet-dragging by Oliver Lyttleton and that, had clothes rationing been introduced six months earlier, it would not have needed to be so stringent. Lyttleton had actually tried to introduce clothes rationing earlier, but this had been vetoed most emphatically by Churchill.

Some retailers did well; second-hand shops saw a boom, as did dry-cleaners, invisible menders and shoe repairers. Hatters did well; instead of a new outfit, an old one brightened up with a new (unrationed) hat, was just the thing. Fur dealers also did well, as animal skins were not rationed, and dress-hire became the thing for formal occasions among the well-to-do. Among the losers were glove makers (who was going to waste coupons on what were optional extras?), bridal and formal outfitters, and those with large stocks of mackintoshes, which needed a quarter of your annual allocation of coupons, and could be replaced by an umbrella.

Playing the system became a national pastime. People latched upon non-rationed alternatives, such as material that could be made up into clothes. At first there was nothing to stop retailers with large pre-rationing stocks of high coupon-value items such as overcoats or raincoats getting rid of them by claiming that they were second-hand and therefore coupon-free, but maximum prices were soon established above which second-hand clothing and shoes would need coupons.

On June 1, 1942, the ration book for 1942/3 was issued. It was a small, grey affair, containing just 60 coupons for the next fourteen months. There were also supplementary sheets of ten coupons for children or workers in certain jobs, or twenty or thirty coupons for older children. In March 1943 the original expiry date of the 1942/3 book, July 31, was extended to August 31, making a twelve-monthly total of forty-eight coupons. In May 1943 it was announced that the annual coupon allowance was once again to be cut. The 1943/4 book was red, a colour that would remain until the end of clothes rationing in 1949. Another innovation was the introd-uction of Children's and Junior Books, containing the appropriate number of coupons, thus saving much time and effort claiming and doling out sheets of extra coupons. In 1944, rations were increased to forty-eight coupons.

In May 1944, **Mother** magazine commented: *'Rationing has helped a lot. It has levelled us, for we all know that no matter what differences there may be in our purses or our ideas, in this business of coupons we are dead equal. For our babies we have 60 and not one more. Nor can we buy much more than the one quality, and to get anything in the way of quantity we are dependent, one upon the other, on what we can borrow or beg from our neighbours.'*

At first, lost coupons could be replaced and loose coupons redeemed, so a thriving black market sprang up. Some, especially the least well off, did not use all their coupons, and few objected to their selling their

▼ Typical Board of Trade newspaper advertisement from late 1943 for Make Do and Mend Classes.

ISSUED BY THE BOARD OF TRADE

BOARD OF TRADE

A 'good turn' saves 18 coupons

A tweed suit, shabby and rather faded, was brought to a Make-do and Mend class not long ago. " As the material is still good, I was thinking of turning it. Could you show me how ? " asked the owner. The instructions she was given may help you—here they are.

1 With a small pair of scissors, unpick seams in following order : Armhole seams, collar joins, hems, main side seams, shoulders. Unpick facings, darts and buttonholes, remove pockets, placket facings, buttons and fastenings. Unpick sleeve seams and take off cuffs.

2 Pull out cut threads. Brush each part thoroughly. Press with hot iron and damp cloth.

3 Tack and stitch garment together as though making new, but reversing each piece.

The left sleeve becomes the right and vice versa. Coat fronts are reversed. New buttonholes must be made on opposite side.

Buttonholes must be neatly sewn up and the buttons sewn on over them.

Placket must be brought to the other side of the skirt.

NEEDLES SIMPLY FLY AT
MAKE-DO AND MEND CLASSES—
for sewing is much easier when you have help and company. Why not join a class ? Your local Evening Institute, Technical College or Women's Organisation are probably running one now. Or ask at the Citizens' Advice Bureau—they'll tell you where and when these classes meet.

remaining coupons. Forged clothing coupons made newspaper headlines in July 1941, just one month after clothing rationing had been introduced. These were being sold by touts in the West End at 10/- a sheet. They proved most easy to fake, as by the very scale of the rationing operation, they were of a fairly simple design, and few people looked twice at them. Illegal printers who had previously turned out forged money found they could make a bigger profit by turning their attention to coupons. The scale of the operation was huge: by February 1942, almost 100,000 forged coupons had been seized. By May 1942, the going bulk rate for genuine (stolen) coupons was £11 a thousand, though by the end of the war the prices of forged coupons were about five times this amount. In 1944, the black market value of a clothing book had risen to £5, from just 2/6 in 1941, while individual coupons had gone up from 3d to 3/- each.

One of the results of the Limitation of Supplies Orders, which restricted the amount

of goods a manufacturer could produce, was that many tended to concentrate on the production of higher priced goods, on which profits were higher. Subsequently many cheaper items of clothing became practically unobtainable. To overcome this the Board of Trade introduced the Utility scheme. The aim of the scheme was to ensure that a range of all essential articles of clothing should be made to simple specifications which, by standardisation, coupled with the absence of purchase tax on Utility clothing, would keep costs low. The initial designs for the clothes and fabrics were produced by leading designers of the time, their brief being to produce garments which used the minimum of materials and labour but were well made and appealing.

The absence of purchase tax made the scheme attractive to the public, and therefore to manufacturers. The first stage was Utility fabric, made to very strict specifications, using small pattern repeats to minimise waste in matching up. Manufacturers were prohibited from making up Utility fabrics into other than Utility garments. The next stage of the scheme was to draw up a series of categories of clothing, with maximum prices for each category. Unfortunately, at first, there was no specification of quality, and some early Utility products were so poor as to jeopardise the reputation of the scheme. Some remained so – Utility shoes were never loved.

Soon, however, precise specifications were drawn up. Sizes and the quantity and quality of materials used were regulated. When the Board of Trade was satisfied that the manufacturer had conformed to all the regulations, their product could be described as Utility and the Utility mark attached to it. This became perhaps the best known symbol of the War – CC41 – standing for Civilian Clothing 1941, introduced in September 1941, although the scheme grew to cover far more than just clothing. The mark was intended to be a sign of quality at a fair price.

▾ Cartoon by Sillince. It was not unusual for the less well-off to exchange their coupons for good-quality used clothing. The Woman's look of delight says it all!

" Now, if the lady's 'usband was to 'ave an ol' suit an' overcoat an' a pair o' boots and p'raps an ol' 'at—I 'ave 'ere me card o' clothin' coupons wot I ain't got a lot o' use for"

RE-ENACTORS

Often re-enactors look wrong because their clothes are just too good! Remember clothes rationing meant people usually wore clothes which were old, faded, and repaired. You can be more accurate, and save money, by buying damaged clothes and then 'Make Do and Mend' (see next chapter). This very useful advice on buying second-hand is from the wartime book *Sew and Save*: '*you should look at the underarms and the neck-line of anything you*

may choose. If these are worn you cannot do very much with them. If the fabric of the garment is good, don't let shabby trimmings worry you. Pockets, neck-trimmings, missing buttons can all be replaced. You will not only save money this way, but often get a better-styled, better-made garment than a new one at the same price. This applies particularly to overcoats and suits.' And, we might add, you will look more authentic.

The Board of Trade asked eight top designers – Digby Morten, Worth, Hardy Amies, Norman Hartnell, Bianca Mosca, Peter Russell, Victor Stiebel and Creed, to design

the yard was Utility. The term became synonymous with the word austerity – clothes of good quality, perhaps, but clothes which had to last because you would not be able to

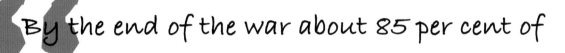

> By the end of the war about 85 per cent of all civilian clothing and materials sold by the yard was Utility

▼ The Utility symbol CC41 standing for Civilian Clothing 1941, although it was sometimes called the two cheeses.

four basic outfits conforming to the regulations of the Utility scheme, including a top coat, suit, afternoon dress and a cotton overall dress. As a result, the Board had a total of thirty-two outfits from which to choose the most suitable to be mass-produced. These were in the shops in Spring 1942.

They were a surprising success. Many had viewed the idea of government approved clothing with more than a little trepidation, but as the 1945 booklet, **Civilian Supplies in Wartime Britain**, said: '*In fact, the customer still has a wide range of choice in most kinds of materials and finished garments, but sizes and the quantity and quality of materials used are regulated ... the mark is thus a guarantee to the consumer of a certain standard of quality.*'

By the end of the war about 85 per cent of all civilian clothing and materials sold by

replace them for a year or two. This could be borne in the name of the war effort, but when rationing and austerity persisted long after hostilities ceased, it became inevitable that the baby of Utility would be thrown out with the bath water of austerity just as soon as possible.

MAKE DO & MEND

Coupons could be stretched in a number of ways, leaving aside illegal methods, such as the black market, or buying 'buckshee' coupons, either stolen or forged. You could buy material or wool to make up into garments, remodel old clothes, or repair worn or damaged clothes. These became known collectively as Make do and Mend.

For the poorer sections of the nation, patching and mending old clothes, passing them down from older to younger siblings or cousins, had always been the way, but the dearth of clothes in the shops in the latter half of 1940 and the beginning of 1941, coupled with rapid increases in prices, meant that more and more people acquired the habit.

The introduction of clothes rationing in June 1941 meant that women who would never have dreamt of mending clothes before the war now did so. These middle and upper-class women had little idea where to start, and the Board of Trade responded by setting up the Make do and Mend campaign. This was 'designed not merely to revive the lost arts of darning and patching, but to raise morale by showing how old clothes can be turned into really smart and attractive new ones.' A plethora of leaflets, well-meaning,

ISSUED BY THE BOARD OF TRADE

8 COUPONS SAVED

—and it all started with two old coats!

Here's Judy's new school frock, nearly finished. Mother made it from a serge coat Judy had worn two summers ago, plus her old flannel blazer. Mother really wasn't much of a dressmaker—but she went to a Make-do and Mend class where she got just the help she needed.

FROM THE BLAZER
Bodice top and sleeves were cut from this material after it had been unpicked and washed.

FROM THE COAT
Unpicking and pressing came first—then the skirt, belt, collar and cuffs were cut out.

PERHAPS YOU'RE AN EXPERT YOURSELF?
Then your help is badly needed by those not as clever with their needles. Give a hand to your next door neighbour or ask a local Women's Organisation how you can help them.

▸ Children's clothes were a particularly good focus for make do and mend, as it is obviously easier to cut down clothes to a smaller size, and growing children, even with extra coupons, were difficult to clothe.

CHART LEAFLET No. 2   ISSUED BY THE BOARD OF TRADE

HOW TO PATCH AN OVERALL

by

Mrs. SEW-and-SEW

Mrs. Sew-and-Sew. A cartoon character introduced by the Board of Trade late in the war to spice up their leaflets.

Patching material for an overall may be cut from the lining of yoke, belt, pocket, .cuffs or collar. The sleeves and hem could be shortened: If you are patching patterned material, always match design perfectly and hem very neatly and the result will be almost invisible. Contrasting cloth can be used to replace a part that is cut away, and pieces of the overall can be put by for future patching but sometimes a little dull, were produced. In 1944, the cartoon character 'Mrs. Sew-and-Sew', appeared in the Board's adverts in newspapers and women's magazines. It also produced short films and, with the help of education authorities and women's voluntary organisations, set up Make do and Mend classes; by the end of the war, 50,000 such classes were meeting regularly. It also organised advice centres, where women could consult experts, many of these were set up in the larger stores, while mobile versions travelled round factory canteens, so workers could get information during their lunch breaks. The Board's booklet, **Make do and Mend**, became a best-seller, selling 1.25 million copies.

Publishers and magazines responded with their own books and articles full of advice and patterns, along with competitions for their readers' best tips; suddenly it was not only necessary, but fashionable to be seen in remodelled and patched clothes in what had become a show of patriotism: *'Nowadays, every re-made garment becomes a uniform of honour and every darn a "decoration."'* **Home Companion**, July 1943.

'Patched elbows these days are no disgrace, of course, but while we're on the job, there's no reason why we shouldn't be cunning, is there? And my particular little bit of cunning is to reverse the sleeves in your old jumper. Right sleeve goes into left arm-hole and vice-versa. Result is that both patches come on the inside of the arm where they can't be seen and furthermore there's going to be far less strain on 'em there.' **Home Companion**, August 1943.

Soon Make do and Mend exhibitions were everywhere from village halls to London stores: *'I saw such a pretty waistcoat the other day, and it hadn't cost a single coupon because it was made from all sorts of odd bits of materials – tiny scraps that most people wouldn't think of bothering with – before clothes' rationing. Now, put into a patchwork design, they made one of the cheeriest garments ever.'* **Home Companion,** 1943.

Even in these times, if you could afford it, dressmakers and tailors would make up material to your preferred designs.

Hutton's of Northern Ireland advertised *'New Clothes Without Coupons – Let Hutton's Fashion specialists remodel your "last-season's" coat into a delightful two-piece suit ... Or let our dressmaking department make up your own material to copy any desired model.'* While advertisements in **Vogue** and other fashion magazines included: *'Blouses without coupons – we make old shirts or your own material into smart blouses at 2 guineas each.'* And: *'As you cannot go to Paris come to Margaret Mangin (French) where you will find Parisian taste and work. Robes et Manteaux and remodelling and customer's own materials made up.'* Or: *'Anita Bodley will make up your own material into dresses, coats and suits with a distinctly American touch.'* And, of course: *'Gentlemen's suits converted into*

spring tailor-mades.' You could even have knitting done: *'Specially designed jumpers from your own yarns from 5 guineas.'*

Bespoke, professional dressmaking was still subject to austerity provisions. Clothing patterns usually had printed on them: *'Professional dressmakers are reminded that they must comply with the Making of Civilian Clothing (Restriction) Orders'.*

The list of conversions was endless: *'a chintzy bedspread from the spare room made a flowery dirndl skirt to wear about the house. The left-over bits made two snappy little buster suits for a wee man, and the snippets made most attractive padded and quilted gardening gloves. A new Peter Pan collar for your winter frock out of an old felt hat.*

'Make yourself the snappiest little stripey shirt blouses from hubby's old pyjama jackets! Blue and white stripes go with a navy suit, candy pink, maroon and white stripes team up wonderfully with grey, and plain blue poplin goes with almost anything, as *Few things are smarter on a woman than a blouse made of men's shirting.*

'Every old or obsolete garment can be used to make something else. Old evening and party dresses can be converted into attractive lingerie and nighties. Old frocks combined to make fashionable new ones. Out of date suits, turned, shortened and brought up to date. Worn out raincoats made into dungarees for the children, the check linings making attractive shirts and blouses to match. Old blankets, worn in patches, make attractive and warm dressing gowns.'* **101 Ways to Save Money in Wartime.**

A Board of Trade advertisement from March 1943, suggested: *'Out of an old sheet, which was only worn in parts, I made two shirts with undetachable collars. Also, out of remnants of other sheets, I got six pairs of shorts for him, using the elastic from the tops of his old ones – also, there was enough material to make six soft collars, a dozen*

handkerchiefs, and several table napkins and pillow slips.'

The importance of preparing material for re-use was emphasised: *'Remember when unpicking old garments to make new ones, to unpick the seams, wash the material, and press the pieces flat before recutting. Then use a reliable pattern for the new garment you wish to make.'* **101 Ways to Save Money in Wartime.**

It was important to be choosy in the bits you re-used: *'When we plan new clothes from old, let's see that the worn parts of the old don't turn up doing the same job on the new. Don't put elbows or under-arms in the same place again. These, together with the "seat", are best left out of the garment altogether.'*

'The insides of the pockets of machine-knitted cardigan make the grandest patches for underarms that are worn and elbows that are torn. A perfect match, and so, of course, the mend is well and truly invisible! An odd scrap of silk lines the denuded pocket and the cardigan gets given six months more to live!' **War Time Needlework.**

The book, **Sew & Save**, gave instructions on how to make a Smart Skirt From An Old Coat, and possibly a bolero jacket as well: *'The parts you'll want to use for the skirt will be the parts that are least worn. If it is faded, turn the material inside out. Cut the skirt from a basic pattern, placing the pieces so that the hem of the skirt comes a little above where the hem of the coat had been. Hems are apt to fray, and the turn-up of the coat hem may have become worn. So it is wise not to have the hem of your new skirt in exactly the same place. If your coat had a flared line, you will of course find it easier to make a flared or gored skirt. If it was a perfectly straight coat, make a straight skirt with an inverted pleat in front.*

'After you have made your skirt, there is still enough of the coat left at the top for a sleeveless bolero. Take out the sleeves and remove any fur or

trimming there may have been at the neck-line. Then cut straight across the back, and in a rounded curve where the two fronts meet, turn under and hem.'

Many of the clothes to be converted were from the wardrobe of the (often absent) man of the house: *'Suppose you can beg an old checked flannel shirt from hubby – if you can you're in luck, because you can cut it down into the neatest little "lumber jacket" for yourself. Take it in where needs be, shorten the sleeves, cut off the tail and from this make four neat little flap pockets and a tie-on girdle. Just the thing to wear with slacks and low-heeled shoes, and if it's an idea that doesn't appeal to you, it certainly will to your teen-year old daughter.'* **Home Companion**, June 1943.

'A pair of man's trousers that has become shiny can be cut up and made into a skirt for yourself. Unpick the seams at the inside of the legs, open the material out, sponge away any stains, and press it. Then place your skirt pattern so that the waist part falls towards the trouser turn-up (the narrow part in both cases), and the fullness at the hem is provided for by the top waist of the trousers.' **Sew and Save**.

And: *'Borrow a couple of hubby's raciest peace-time hankies and see what attractive raglan sleeves they make for your very plain working frock! What you do is shorten the sleeves of this old-timer, then stitch the hankies over them so that one of the points dips to the elbow and its opposite number comes high up to the neck. Turn the other two points in till you get the correct shape, then cut, pin and stitch. The left over bits will make neat little pockets to swagger on either hip.'* **Home Companion**, October 1943.

Using non-rationed materials for making and mending meant saving on coupons. At first, light furnishing fabrics and curtain material were used, so these were soon added to the list of rationed goods. They were replaced by dust sheets and even funeral shrouds. During the war black-out material was coupon-free, and therefore a good source, but in September 1945, it too went on coupons.

'Unpick those sacks, wash them, dye them a warm dark red, and then the fun begins. Choose a frock pattern with a simple flared skirt and plain little bodice – the button-into "overall" frock is the ideal pattern to aim at. Once cut out and stitched together,

it's up to you to take away the frock's homely look by gaying it up. Patch-pockets, and collar and cuffs in bright green felt, is one notion, and another is bright flowers embroidered down the front, over the pockets and round the cuffs. And none of your fine needle-work here ladies. Something big and splashy and quickly done in coarse thread is the idea. Pink and bright speedwell blue flowers would look lovely on dark red, wouldn't they?' **Home Companion**, November 1943. A similar source was flour bags which could be boiled to take the lettering out. Alternatively, you could knit jumpers from unrationed dishcloth yarn.

▼ Absent men proved an excellent source of materials for make do and mend. Many came back from the war to find their wardrobes empty!

Skirt Pattern No. 20,117.
Jacket Pattern No. 20,116.

Your New Suit from **HIS OLD ONE**

Not everyone approved. One reader of **Woman** magazine wrote: *'It has been deemed necessary, apparently by experts, for the government to ration clothes. Therefore why do so many people – and publications – plot and scheme to evade the rationing? A magazine I read recently has an article in it telling one how to make "couponless" clothes out of blackout material, bedspreads, rugs, blankets and many other essential house furnishings. Surely if we take advantage of these rather despicable schemes, we are merely asking for more restrictions on these hitherto uncontrolled goods? And why cheat, anyway?'* The editor replied: *'Evading regulations has always been a human hobby, since humans invented regulations. We think, though, that your point about the spread of rationing is a sound one.'*

and could be used for children's clothes or hospital supplies.

'In many sheep-rearing districts children brought in wool from the hedges to be washed, spun and knitted by the local housewives. At Hailsham appreciable quantities of good wool were obtained from the combings of pet dogs and cats.'

Home Companion, of January 1943, reported: *'The various women's organisations staged a show of their handiwork in London recently and exhibits [included] gloves spun and woven from Pekinese hairs.'*

Knitting became such a facet of wartime civilian life that one wartime housewife, Bessie Palmer, summed up the home front as 'knitting and queuing'. Every woman's

> "Firemen and ARP workers would struggle to make mines safe before the bomb-disposal teams got to them; the reward was the equivalent of many pairs of silk knickers!"

Silk was in demand for war purposes, especially for parachutes. In 1941, its use for stockings and civilian clothing was banned. If you knew someone who worked in a parachute factory you might get remnants, otherwise the only source for civilians was German land mines, which were dropped on green silk parachutes, some of which became entangled on their descent. Firemen and ARP workers would struggle to make the mines safe before the bomb-disposal teams got to them; the reward was the equivalent of many pairs of silk knickers!

Women In Green, the official history of the Women's Voluntary Services, notes that: *'Materials which could be used in clothing or as household linens were recovered from unusual sources. Special appeals were made for drawings on linen to be turned out by architects and engineers' offices, and very large numbers of these were boiled till the fine linen base was freed from the paper surface*

magazine had directions to knit something, and there were a myriad of books with titles such as **Knitting in Wartime**.

The war had hardly started when people were exhorted to knit 'comforts' for the services. Scarves, hats, gloves, jumpers and

◀ (opposite) An often-worn dress could be transformed by the addition of a home-made collar and cuff set, made from felt or other odds and ends.

▸ Crocheted scarves. We mostly think of the war in terms of knitting, but many wartime make do and mend items were, like these scarves, crocheted.

▸ Men's Cranwell front from **Knitting for the RAF** published 1939. The Cranwell front was a cross between a polo-neck jumper and a scarf. At the beginning of the war, knitting 'comforts' for the Forces was the patriotic thing to do.

MEN'S CRANWELL FRONT
IN 4-PLY WOOL

MATERIALS : 3 ozs. of R.A.F. knitting wool, 4-ply, and two No. 7 knitting needles.

TENSION : 5 sts. to 1 inch.

MEASUREMENTS : Depth from shoulder 6½ inches ; width across lower edge, 14 inches.

THE BACK :
Cast on 76 sts. and work in garter st. (K. every row) for 6½ inches. To shape shoulders, cast off 4 sts. at the beginning of each of the next 8 rows (44 sts. remain). Now work in k. 2, p. 2 ribbing for 8 inches. Cast off loosely ribwise.

THE FRONT :
Work exactly as given for the back.

TO MAKE UP :
Press each piece lightly on the wrong side under a damp cloth, but do not flatten the ribbing. Join the shoulder seams and side seams of collar.

6½"

14"

Old knitted garments could be unravelled and reused. The Board of Trade advised: *take pains in unravelling. It's half the battle. Careful washing will take out the crinkles – tight winding won't. Here are some hints:*

1. Unpick seams. Unravel the knitting, winding the wool round a tray, or a dressbox lid.
2. Tie it into skeins using several knots.
3. Wash the skeins in lukewarm suds, squeezing gently until the wool is clean. Rinse twice in water of the same temperature.
4. Dry skeins by stringing them together and pegging them on a line or hanging on two hooks. It's best to dry outdoors. Shake gently now and then to prevent tangling.
5. Wind into loose balls and re-knit.

Remember that the wool will not go as far a second time. This may mean short instead of long sleeves or a jumper instead of a cardigan

> # "With everything so tight, waste was unforgivable, and destructive pests had to be exterminated mercilessly"

balaclava helmets were the most common items; comforts funds were set up, and schools 'adopted' regiments or ships to knit for.

With rationing, people were knitting for themselves. Knitting-wool was rationed: *'The number of coupons required for hand knitting yarn containing more than 16 per cent by weight of wool is one coupon for every 2 ounces'*, but fewer coupons were required to buy the wool to make a sweater or a pair of socks than would be needed if the article were purchased already made-up.

Alternatively you might try ...

RENEWING WITHOUT UNDOING

Put in a strip-patch to replace worn underarm or thin elbows. Matching or contrasting colour can be used.

1. **Unpick seam and pull a thread out right across. Unravel worn part and pick up stitches.**
2. **Knit in a new strip.**
3. **Graft last row of patch to garment or oversew loops together from wrong side. Be careful not to miss a loop.**

It became increasingly difficult to buy enough wool in one colour to knit a whole jumper or whatever. The answer was fairisle, being made up of small amounts of several different colours.

'Amusing patch pockets made from an oddment of cherry or jade-coloured wool! Knit them for your dreariest Autumn frock – a breast-pocket and a swaggering hip-pocket – and team them up with a coloured leather belt to match.' **Home Companion**, May 1943.

'There's nothing like a good pressing to keep you interested in your clothes. Instead of using an ordinary damp cloth when you press, by the way, make a point of dipping the cloth in ammonia and water. It will freshen up the garment tremendously, and you'll find you manage to remove quite a few stains in the process.' Or, for a shiny shirt back: *'Use a clean rag, dab gently at the shine with the turps, then air-off the garment out of doors.'* **Home Companion.** Or: *'Rub leaky spots on last year's raincoat with beeswax. Lay a sheet of brown paper on and press with a warm iron.'* **Home Companion**, November 1943.

If clothes had to last longer, it was essential to keep them clean. **101 Ways to Save Money in Wartime** advised: *'Dissolve an ounce of glue in a pint jug of water on the stove. Fill a bath with hot water and stir in the thoroughly dissolved glue solution. Then put the blanket or garment in the bath, stirring occasionally. Leave for about half an hour, when all the dirt will come out. Put the article through the wringer, then rinse again in water of the same temperature, and wring again in a dry towel. when nearly dry, press.'* Which sort of glue is unspecified and it would NOT be a good idea to experiment with this on treasured original garments – perhaps try some old rags first.

Other home-made renovations included a tablespoonful of concentrated ammonia in one pint of warm water; this mixture was recommended to freshen dark clothes, the surface of which were brushed lightly with the solution, using a nail brush. A weak solution made from used tea leaves could be used to soak a black frock gone rusty before washing.

The shine could be removed from very heavy cloths such as those used for overcoats, by using the finest grade sandpaper to raise a new surface. While an old silk frock could be cleaned with warm sudsy water, then rinsed

No. 440 Man's CARDIGAN

No. 529 OUTDOOR SET for two-year-old boy

No. 562 HOOD, ANKLE SOCKS and GLOVES

No. 572 JUMPER-CARDIGAN

No. 619 Two Pairs of Men's SOCKS

several times in clear water, adding a little drop of vinegar to the last one. The frock would then be dried rolled up in a clean towel, not pegged out, and ironed while still very damp. Another useful tip, this time to prevent men's ties loosing their shape when washed, was to thread a fine needle with silk and tack it down each side, taking in the inside stiffening with the stitches. You could then wash and dry it, then remove the tacking threads, keeping the tie absolutely flat, and press it with a hot iron over a damp cloth.

▸ A few of the vast range of accessories which you could make yourself, including slippers, collars, hat pins and so on.

▾ Underclothing was an area ripe for make do and mend work. If the results were not perfect, they would not be on public display, and coupons could thus be saved for items that were.

'Mackintoshes are cleaned with cold water and soap solution. If your mac is very dirty, soak it overnight in a large tub with 2ozs. of dissolved borax, which will loosen the dirt. Then you can scrub it with a soft brush. It should be hung up to dry on a hanger without squeezing the water out of it first, as you must be careful not to crease the rubber. A rubber mac cannot, of course, be ironed, so pull it and smooth it out with your hands as it gradually dries. If you have grease stains on a mackintosh, try rubbing fuller's earth into them, leaving for some time, and then removing the absorbed grease gently with your finger-nails.' **101 Ways to Save Money in Wartime**.

'Skirts don't get that baggy "sat out" look if they're half-lined at the back, and box-pleats stay down when they're pegged down with paper clips for the night. All-round pleats stay in position if the edges of the pleats are stitched down, and hats keep their shape if they're stuffed out with paper when they're not on the wearer's head.' **Home Companion**, May 1943. Or: *'Katie's daughter's black gym stockings*

ISSUED BY THE BOARD OF TRADE

How to Save 5 coupons on UNDIES

" I searched my scrap bag," said Mrs. A.' " I had a good many ' bits and pieces ' and at the Make-do and Mend class they showed me how to cut knickers from these old scraps of material, joining the gores in alternating colours."

" I cut down a frock that was too small," said Mrs. B. " Took the top off, you see ; put on shoulder straps and shaped the skirt to make camiknicks. I've another frock that I'm going to turn into a blouse with knickers attached."

COME ONCE— and you'll come again

Whatever your sewing problems, a Make-do and Mend class will help you. Your local Evening Institute, Technical College or Women's Organisation is probably running a class now ; or ask at the Citizens' Advice Bureau—they'll be able to tell you about times and places.

have a neat square of strong black net stitched into the backs of the heels before they're worn. It strengthens, and when the hole does eventually come, darning over the net makes the mend a doubly lasting one.' **Home Companion**, July 1943.

With everything so tight, waste was unforgivable, and destructive pests had to be exterminated mercilessly. Under these circumstances, moths became flying public enemy number two, just after the Luftwaffe.

'Summer finery gets tucked away till next year – a little soap dissolved in the last rinsing water for your cotton frocks will make them stiff enough to be folded crisply – the hems of children's frocks should be unpicked before washing so that letting down next year will be a simple job. Your own light cardigans and summer-weight suits are best stored hanging up, but pleat and pocket openings should be tacked down, collar revers too. Pad shoulders, and to keep moths away, thread mothballs on a string and hang down each of the sleeves,' and: *'wrap them first in newspaper (because moths hate the smell of printer's ink!) then roll your parcel up in tissue paper gummed well and truly down with sticking paper.'* Further: *'Moths hate the smell of household soap! So when you've chopped up those long bars into cakes do pop them among your blankets and other heavy woollens that you're storing away for the summer months – it'll stop them from going musty, and discourage hearty moth appetites.'* **Home Companion**, June 1943.

Skirts and dresses could be changed by the addition of a little ribbon: *'stitch your ribbon round the foot of the hem – the more colours and rows of ribbon the merrier, and when you walk your skirt will look for all the world like a swinging, dancing rainbow.'* The same idea could be used on the yoke of a dark jumper, or: *'another colourful idea is to stitch material of gay colour over the inside of inverted pleats. When you walk, out springs a gay splash of colour which looks tremendously attractive.'* **Home Companion**, June 1943. Again: *'Contrasting braid zig-zagged around the neck and again across the bodice will give a plain frock a new zest for life. The same idea could be used effectively on a blouse.'* **Home Companion**, April 1943.

Military styles often inspired wartime

BESTWAY
LEAFLET **3**d.
No. 600

PRETTY ACCESSORIES
To Give as Gifts (Only Requiring Oddments)

fashions. Another idea from the same publication suggested the following, adapted from the style of trousers worn by the Royal Marines: *'…a stripe of red braid could be stitched along the underarm sleeves of a black frock, running down to the hem…That cheerful wide stripe hides two darned elbows and two underarm thin places.'*

Here's one from **Sew & Save** for 'military-looking epaulettes' on the shoulder lines of a dress: *'To make tassels, cut a piece of cardboard the depth you want the tassel to be, and wind the wool round and round it about fifteen times. Then knot the strands together at the top, and cut the ends open at the bottom. Take a piece of firm silk of the same colour (or a colour that contrasts well) and wind this several times round the tassel just below the knotted threads at the top to make the head of the tassel. Sew the tassels along the shoulder-line of your dress at regular intervals. About five tassels on each shoulder are enough.'*

Woman's Weekly had a similar idea: *'Buy half a yard of black fringe [unrationed], two or three inches deep, and machine it, top edge to top edge, in a double row along the shoulder seams of your rather plain black frock. And you could have some on the pockets, too!'*

Trimmings could make a huge difference. Bands of a darker material to form a yoke to the bodice and sleeves, to edge the cuffs and form a peplum. **Woman's Weekly** suggested you: *'Rejuvenate your black frock for the evening by cutting the front of the neck fairly low and edging it with a frilled fold of black satin. Add also a wide, soft sash and two gathered folds at the front to give a basque effect.'* Or: *'The answer to a dull little navy frock is a dainty crocheted collar in sugar-pink icing. Crochet pink tops to cover its dull navy buttons and crochet for yourself a dainty snood in a matching pink.'* The **Home Companion's** idea was to: *'Hunt up some strongly contrasting material and treat that old frock to new sleeves (cut raglan style), generous revers and a large pair of patch pockets … Fur or fur-fabric can give a very up-to-the-minute look to even the plainest coat. Cover the collar and outline the lapels and pocket, slits or flaps.*

'Another use for odd pieces of ribbon is to make them into bows. These can be sewn in couples, one above the other, on the edge of a short sleeve or at the front of a belt. To make ribbon bows, fold each end over into the required length and sew flat. Trim the ends. The middle of the bow is then finished by taking a few running-stitches down the centre of it to draw it up, and folding over it another piece of ribbon with a small pleat down the centre. Hem down neatly at the back.' **Sew & Save**.

Woman's Weekly suggested: *'Three velvet bows, graduated in size, worn on the lapel of your coat. Let them match the colour of your sweater.'* **Mother** magazine suggested: *'Two pairs of neat, flat bows to perch on the pockets of a tailored dress. Narrow bows are best for a breast pocket, matching wide ribbon on the hip.'*

'Initials are always an amusing, and obviously personal decoration,' **Sew & Save** suggested: *'An odd piece of felt, highly-coloured woollen material, or stiff bright taffeta can be used to cut your initials from. Whip the edges unless you are using felt, mount the initials on a piece of canvas, or petersham for stiffening, and pin them just below the left-hand shoulder of your dress, on your coat lapel, your bag, or even on the side of your hat.'*

Buttons could change the look of a suit, but like everything else they were not easy to come by: *'Ornamental buttons made from acorns! All you do is polish your acorns till they're shiny bright, then screw a tiny size in picture rings into the base of each to form the shank. And wouldn't they look most wonderfully at home on a nut-brown, or leafy-green jumper?'* **Home Companion**, January 1943.

Alternatively you could cover plain buttons with velvet or some other bright material.

You were likely to have only one outer coat which had to be used for all weathers: *'Service people must be prepared to suffer cold at all times, so we can safely accept some of their ideas in keeping warm. Especially good to me seemed the hint of sewing an ordinary wash-leather across the inside of the back of your jacket, and another in the back of your shirt. Only a firm tack here and there is needed.'* **Woman's Weekly,** December 1944.

101 Ways to Save Money in Wartime suggested: *'If you have not a raincoat, save your coupons and your money for war savings by waterproofing an old coat this way : Prepare a solution as follows. Add 1 ounce of powdered alum and 1 ounce of sugar of lead to a gallon of rainwater. Stir well, then allow to settle and pour off the clear liquid. Immerse the material in this for about four hours. Wring out, dry partially, then put through a mangle or press with a heavy iron. Most materials can be treated in this way with satisfactory results.'*

ACCESSORIES

Wartime restrictions meant that last year's outfit would have to do for this year too, and accessories became the way to freshen a tired wardrobe. New shoes, stockings, hat, scarf and gloves could ring the changes on a top coat, and a change of belts, a headscarf, and some jewellery would add a new look to the frocks. Shoes and stockings were also rationed, although the latter could be knitted. Other accessories were coupon-free, however, the usual limitations and shortages meant that they were often too difficult to come by, and the emphasis was very much on making your own from scraps and recycled or unusual materials.

▶ Teenage girl. Notice everything is hand knitted – scarf, beret and jumper.

SHOES

'Wooden-soled shoes have come on in the world. They are gay and right for any weather' says Mrs. Sew-and-Sew

'Fine coupon value, woodies — especially when looked after properly.' Board of Trade Advert, August 1944.

Shoes were, of course, one of the major accessories. Rationing meant that, as with clothing, fashions in footwear were dictated as much by the limitations of available materials as by controls on manufacturing. The Utility scheme tried to provide well designed, well made items using the minimum of resources but the government admitted that: *'The quality of shoes, especially children's shoes, Rayon stockings and corsets has been very widely criticised.'* Shoes had become flat; in 1942, the heels of women's shoes were limited to a maximum of two inches (if you were lucky), and many women described Utility shoes as 'clumpy'.

Under clothes rationing, a pair of men's boots or shoes would need seven coupons, and women's, five. This meant that it was important to choose sensibly. The **Home Companion** advised its readers that: *'High heels should be resolutely banished except for high days and holidays, and comfortable ones installed in their place. We used to shy away from flat-heeled shoes*

▸ Interesting advert showing the range of colours available in October 1944.

▸ & ▾ Flat-soled shoes. Many of the flat-soled shoes produced in the second half of the war look very modern to our eyes.

JOYCE (CALIFO

because they looked out of place with anything except country clothes, but that doesn't hold good any more. You can wear 1943 flat heels with even the towniest clothes, because they're made so smartly and look so neat and attractive.'

It was important that maximum use should be got out of all clothes, including shoes. The Board of Trade advised people to have two pairs of shoes, worn on alternate days. It was stressed that they should always be cleaned and put on shoe trees at night, and in the absence of these, little balls of newspaper pushed tightly into the shoe would serve.

Reviving worn shoes was important. Brown leather shoes which had become stained should be gently scrubbed with saddle soap and a little tepid water; black kid or glacé shoes wearing grey could be recondi-tioned by the application of a mixture of Indian ink and olive oil, while patent leather shoes should be cleaned with milk and a soft rag, and brightened up with a drop of turpentine. In extremis you could try varnishing them – two coats were recommended. If, of course, you could get the varnish then you might also give the soles a coat to waterproof them, while if you had cracks across the toes of a pair of brown shoes the answer was to paint very sparingly over the cracks with iodine, using a fine brush, and polish them with shoe cream once thoroughly dry.

The main problem with shoes was the shortage of leather to make them, especially the thicker leather needed for the soles. Rubber as an alternative was out; the manufacture of crepe rubber soles and heels was prohibited in 1942. Traditional clogs were one way around these shortages; when rationing was introduced clogs were coupon-free to encourage their use and they soon became an everyday sight.

A variation on clogs were wooden soled shoes, introduced in January 1943. In style they were like flat shoes with a separate heel added to a shaped sole. The uppers were in coloured suede, lace-up style. The three-quarter inch thick platform sole and heel were made from birch or poplar, with the toe curved up at the front to allow a heel-toe action when walking. The soles were edged round with a colour contrasting the uppers. To protect the wood, leather, composition, or reclaimed rubber reinforcements were added, like the sole and heel pieces of ordinary shoes.

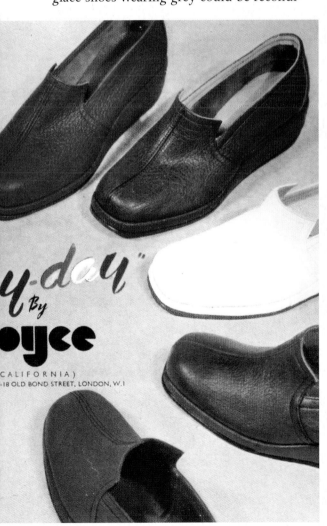

Smart Practical Economical ....Essentially Yours

Dolcis

.... Our new Spring models, cleverly designed by leading stylists, combine all the qualities you have been looking for .... refined smartness, perfect fitting, choice materials and yet .... moderately priced.

Style 9362. Punched Fancy Court in Black, Brown, Wine or Blue Suede - - - - - - - - - - - 32/6

Style 9363. Bow Court with Dutch Heel in Black, Brown, Wine or Blue Calf - - - - - - - - - 40/-

Style 1512. Crepe Sole Tie Shoe in Black, Ice, Brown, Wine, Green or Blue Calf. With contrasting coloured trimmings - - - - - 40/-

Style 9365. Studded Gusset Bow Court in Black, Brown, Wine or Blue Suede - - - - - - - - - 37/6

There is a DOLCIS Shoe Store in every Large Town
Write to Head Office, Dolcis House, Great Dover Street, London, S.E.I. for the nearest Branch address

The Board of Trade announced: *'You'll soon be seeing more and more wooden-soled shoes about the place. They save rubber and leather – both badly needed for direct war purposes – and are snug, well-fitting and waterproof.*

'It's said that the factory and mill workers of the North, who wear wooden-soled clogs, seldom suffer from colds and weak chests, so wooden-soles will be welcome when the winter comes again. When you first put on a pair of these shoes, you'll feel at once how solid and comfortable they are – but you may have to adjust yourself by a little practice to the rolling tread of the rigid wooden sole. It's naturally different to the flexible leather or rubber sole.'

Style on a friendly footing

◀ ▲ A selection of women's shoes from 1942.

Park Lane

.... and these are the three comfort features ....

1. Steel arch support—gives comfort in the right place.

2. Sponge rubber cushion—relieves the forward pressure of high heels.

3. Flat innersole—you walk the way Nature intended.

The **Home Companion** of August, 1943, took up the point: *'We all of us know how to do the Lambeth Walk – but how about the Wooden Sole Walk? It's easy when you do – so if you've bought a pair of shoes with wooden soles, here's the secret. Cultivate the "rolling tread", and this means that from the moment your heel touches the ground you roll forward in your shoe till the tip of the toe is reached. Try it, and practice it, because once you've got it you'll go rolling home feeling as if you're walking on air for a change – and not on*

◂ Men's shoes from 1943.

wood!' By 1945, wooden-soled shoes needed coupons, two a pair, but this still compared well with women's leather-soled shoes, which by then required seven. Men's shoes changed little in style over the war, although rationing meant that more daring styles, such as correspondents shoes, or brogues, requiring unnecessary work, became very rare.

The swift advance of the Japanese forces in Malaya in 1942 meant the loss to Britain of the important rubber plantations. The Ministry of Supply reported that nine out of ten rubber trees were in Japanese hands. What little rubber we had was needed for the services. Consequently wellington boots, rubber gloves, and similar items were almost impossible to get. If they were essential for their job, industrial workers could apply for a buying permit to the Factory Inspectors, and farm workers to their local War Agricultural Committee. Even then you still needed coupons – four for wellingtons, rubber overshoes and rubber bootees, two for ankle-length boots.

Anything that was that hard to get had to be carefully looked after. The leaflet **101 Ways to Save Money in Wartime** said: *'Rubber boots will last twice as long as usual if dried in this way. Keep two stockings filled with bran and tied at the top. When the boots are wet, place the bran stockings inside and leave for a while. The bran will absorb the moisture and the stockings can be dried in the oven and used again and again.'*

The Board of Trade advised: *'Rubber boots and wellingtons are very precious, so only wear them to keep out the wet, and see that the children keep their gumboots for really wet days and never let them wear them for any other purpose.*

'Clean rubber boots with a wet cloth and plain water – soap is unnecessary – and dry thoroughly by wiping – never put them near heat.

NORVIC
Sun Sandals

Bright suede uppers in various shades and wood soles make a perfect match in these gay sun sandals from Norvic. Lovely to look at and a joy to wear. Only four coupons, too !

Trade Mark

NORVIC SHOE COMPANY LIMITED NORWICH

◂ Wooden-soled sun-sandals. Wooden-soled shoes were introduced to counter serious shortages of leather and rubber.

SOCKS & STOCKINGS

'A new use for old lipstick holders – wash out any remains of lipstick, then fill the holder with soap. Carried in the handbag, one of these would prove a boon as an emergency "stop" for laddered stockings.'
Home Chat magazine, August 1944.

Men's socks had been long – at least half way up the calf, but wartime restrictions meant that they became far shorter. On the other hand, the shortage of stockings meant that many women took to wearing socks, especially with slacks, and with good reason. A pair of non-woollen half-hose, or women's ankle socks were only one coupon, and would last far longer than stockings. Further, they could be darned and, of course, you could knit them yourself.

The Board of Trade's **Make Do and Mend leaflet number 2**, dealt with socks: *'Woollen socks should be bought large enough to allow for shrinking. When knitting socks work in a strong cotton threads with the wool at heels and toes.*

'Mend any hole or thin place as soon as it appears. Many large holes in the heels of socks can be mended either by being darned over a scrap of net or by patching with a piece of new knitting – or a piece from an old sock.

'Perspiration tends to rot socks so they should be rinsed frequently – and never boil socks or stockings.'

When rationing was first introduced, all women's stockings were all two coupons a pair. By 1942, woollen stockings were three coupons, others two, while by 1945 the shortage of fully-fashioned stockings led to their being increased from two coupons to three. It was explained that fully-fashioned stockings took two or three times more labour to manufacture, and of course, such labour could

INVISIBLE MENDING FOR LADDERED STOCKINGS

Fig. 1

Professional charges for invisible mending are high. With a little practice you can mend your own runs.

By Beryl Strange

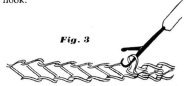

Fig. 2

REAL silk stockings are getting rarer and rarer; even their rayon sisters have a 'coupon-scarcity.' This makes every minor ladder assume the proportions of a major disaster. To turn this into a total triumph, all you need is a little hook and some patience.

This special hook is sold at all big stores under various patent names, such as 'Laddknit.' It costs 7½d. to 1s. 3d. according to where you shop. It is made like the standard hook for rug-making, with a tiny movable arm which covers the point of the hook (Fig. 1).

First catch the bottom stitch of the ladder with needle and thread, so that it cannot run further. Next stretch the laddered part of the stocking over a napkin ring, egg cup, or grooved mending mushroom. Hold with the left hand so that the ladder is firm and straight, but not stretched too tightly (Fig. 2).

Fig. 3.—Catch the first stitch with the hook.

Fig. 3

Fig. 4.—For coarse lisle or rayon, push the hook forward and downward until the movable arm lies between the first stitch and the first thread of the ladder. For fine silk, lift the first thread of the ladder clear; push the hook forward

Fig. 4, lisle

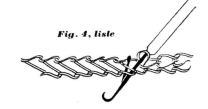

▲ Stockings became so scarce that laddered stockings were sent to the invisible menders, or you could do it yourself, as this article from late 1943 shows.

▼ With clothes rationing stockings became a rare treat. Many women went bare-legged, or used leg make-up like this example.

better be used for the war effort. Later, seamless rayon stockings were reduced from two coupons to one and a half.

By 1944 stockings had become so scarce that the Board of Trade felt it needed to issue this advice: *'If you really need to buy new stockings make sure they're the right size. When buying non-fully-fashioned stockings you will probably need a size larger than with fully-fashioned stockings. When putting on your stockings turn in the toe and gently roll the stocking over the foot and up the leg. Take*

Gloriatan
PERFECT LEG MAKE-UP
with the sheer loveliness of
SILKEN HOSE

Clean, easily applied, harmless dressing.

Will not soil clothes or run in the rain.

Easily removed with soap and water.

Beautiful Legs without stockings

care that rings and fingernails don't catch the threads. Don't suspend stockings too tightly.'

Not only did they become harder to get, but like men's socks, stockings became shorter. **Home Notes** in September 1942 commented: *'Wartime stockings have an annoying habit of being too short. Here's a way to make them longer. Cut the welts off the top of any old, worn-out stocking you have, and stitch them neatly on to the tops of the new stockings. This gives them length, and will feel much more comfortable.'*

If you could get stockings, they had to be made to last. The usual tips were forthcoming: the toes often went first, but this could be avoided by putting a small piece of cotton wool into the toe of each stocking before putting it on, while on a similar note it was pointed out that the big toe tended to poke through unfashioned stockings. This could be avoided if you knitted toe caps, like half a glove finger. These were worn on the toe, under the stocking, and, you were assured, would not only much extend the life of the stockings, but also make them more comfortable to wear.

The Board of Trade, working on the old principle of a stitch in time, reported: *'Worth knowing is a tip about darning two sizeable circles for the suspender grips. Saves wear and tear. For the same reason, single-darn heel and toe and run a double row of machine stitching round the tops of your stockings before ever they're worn'*, but when the inevitable happened: *'leaving the laddered ones at the invisible menders is often a matter of weeks and months before you get them back, but if the ladders aren't too wide, you can make a useful job of repairing them at home. All you do is turn your stockings inside out, bring the laddered seams neatly together, and seam them in with your sewing machine.'* The idea of taking a laddered pair of stockings to be mended seems amazing to us now!

As stockings came in pairs, the **Home Companion** suggested: *'it's a wise woman who now buys her stockings all the same shade, but even so, most of us have got a whole heap of odd stockings left over from better days when we were fancy-free — and surely in that heap are as many different colours* *as in Joseph's own coat! Thing to do, of course, is to match up those stockings for texture, and let a fourpenny stocking-dye team them up for colour! Let the stocking-dye be a couple of shades darker than the darkest "odd man", and you just can't go wrong!'*

In extremis you might try knitting your own. One magazine suggested you might knit fishnet stockings out of hosiery yarn, though most publications suggested using wool. The black market was always an alternative but most of the stockings available through that channel were actually seconds, or rejects put into fake expensive packaging.

Another alternative was to go without stockings altogether. In May 1942, the government asked women to do so in the summer months. This was a good time to go without stockings, but it was pointed out that bare pink and white legs don't look particularly attractive, and getting a tan takes time. Leg make-up provided one answer, either ready-made, or home-made versions using onion skins or gravy browning to dye the legs – attractive to dogs as well as men. One 1943 advertisement for leg cream contains the following advice: *'here's a tip for stockingless legs. If you can't buy stocking make-up, sponge the legs with a few grains of permanganate of potash dissolved in warm water. Be sure to test on the sole of one foot first because it won't wash off for days. Do this before a special occasion on which you want to look your nicest.'*

If you couldn't get leg make-up you might try sun-tan lotion, or even ordinary make-up. First rub in a little cream of any kind, then powder your legs thoroughly with the darkest shade of powder you could get. It was stressed that this would soon wear off and also mark the hem of a dark frock, but for emergencies, and to wear with a washable frock, it was a good makeshift. Fully fashioned stockings had a seam at the back, and this could be reproduced with an eye-brow pencil. Most women found the whole thing

unsatisfactory; leg make-up was often blotchy, and you needed someone with a good eye to draw a straight seam.

Looks aside, going stocking-less had another disadvantage, the **Home Companion** of July 1943 singled out: *'shoes that scrape and rub your poor little feet because lack of coupons sends you out stocking-less this summer! You walk along the burning pavements like a cat on hot bricks, the insoles of your shoes are sticking hard to your bare feet and on the back of your left heel you've got the father and mother of a blister coming. Frankly you're hot and bothered and bad-tempered, but you'd be none of these things if you'd use the feet of old silk stockings to make for yourself cool little 'sockettes' to pop inside your shoes. Use the foot part of the stocking only, cut the instep right away, hem round the top, then thread it through with eyeglass elastic and the "socks" are a perfect fit. Can't be seen, but what a difference they make!'*

Make Do and Mend Leaflet number 2 pointed out that: *'Perspiration ruins boots and shoes. Before going out in hot weather sprinkle dusting powder sparingly inside the shoes themselves if stockings are not being worn. Take off your shoes as soon as you get home and bathe your feet in cold water.'*

Another trick was to put blotting paper soles in your shoes when you went stockingless.

▼ If you could get hold of stockings, extra care was needed to avoid ladders, and this advert from May 1943 gives a few tips on the subject.

(Overleaf) Many DIY magazines and books gave patterns for knitting your own stockings, such as these.

Extra Wear from your Rayon Stockings

Follow these Coupon-Saving Tips

Buy wisely
Get your correct foot size—that's important.

Put on carefully
Turn inside out and slip foot on—roll up smoothly. Don't suspender too tightly.

Wash frequently
Wash after every wearing. Handle carefully when wet. Dry away from direct heat. Don't wear until really dry.

Avoid ladders
Yes, you can avoid ladders. Watch out for the snags—a rough edge on your office desk, a bracelet, ring or shoe buckle. Never an unnecessary ladder must be your "duration" motto.

HATS

Hats were not rationed but women's hats became increasingly expensive as war went on, and as such were increasingly replaced by head scarves, snoods and turbans, while because of material shortages the crowns and brims of men's hats became smaller, hat bands narrower, and the felt coarser.

The great majority of men's hats were either variations on the trilby or cloth cap. Caps were worn extensively by the working class for most occasions, and as casual or sports wear by the better off. These were bigger than those worn today.

The trilby had a high crown and usually a 2 inch wide band. Other hats, such as the bowler or homberg could also be seen, usually worn by older men of the middle or upper classes, although in the building trade the bowler was the symbol of the foreman, or craftsman. With austerity, the felt became rougher, crowns became smaller, as did bands, shrinking to about 1/2 inch wide. Even the flat cap, in its Utility form, became smaller.

Women's hats continued to change for some time. In part, this was because headgear, except for scarves, was not rationed, so a new hat if you could afford it could go a long way to cheer up last year's outfit: *'Small, neat hats are much more fashionable than elaborate affairs with a lot of trimming.'* **Home Notes,** December 1939.

'Every girl seems to be wearing a flared off-the-face brimmed hat. So the hat shops report. The favourites are felt hats faced back with velvet, either black or coloured. But sometimes the facing back is done with fur fabric, of which ocelot is first favourite. Ocelot is that small-spot fur which looks like miniature leopard. All spotted furs are being liked this year.' **Woman and Home,** December 1940.

UP-TO-DATE STYLES

Typical numbers from our New Range to sell at Popular Prices

The SPITFIRE

The WHITLEY

The WELLINGTON

▲ A range of men's hats with appropriate wartime names (the Spitfire, Whitley, and Wellington were all RAF aircraft).

A favourite style of the period was a hat shaped rather like a man's trilby, but with a miniature crown. These were usually worn perched on the front of the head. Later fashions included skull caps, sailor caps, butcher's-boy hats, berets, and even fezzes. Traditional styles that may have featured plumage imported from Europe were more likely to feature feathers from domestic birds, often dyed to match the hat.

and then with tailor's chalk divide the circle up into eight equal parts. This is done by drawing a line with a ruler straight through the middle of the circle, from top to bottom, then another one crossing it from side to side The circle is now divided into quarters; bisect these so that they are in eighths.

'At the far edge of the circle, and exactly on these eight points, make darts about 4 inches deep and 1 to 1½ inches across. These darts shape the underside of the beret. Sew up the darts, then fit the edge of the

▸ A selection of women's hats from March 1940.

As women went to work in factories and industries such as engineering, hats increasingly had a practical as well as decorative function, keeping hair out of the way of machinery. By the middle of the war, many traditional styles in hats were replaced by headscarves, snoods and turbans.

Berets had originally been worn by young girls and boys, but the style had been taken up enthusiastically in the twenties by young women. The popularity of military styling at the beginning of the war made them popular again.

Sew & Save showed how to make a beret from one piece of material: *'Take your head measurements by putting a tape-measure … round the top of the forehead, and meeting just above the nape of the neck. This gives you the fitting of the underside for the beret.*

'Cut out a circle about 10 inches in diameter,

underside into double binding cut to the length of the head measurement already taken.'

Home Companion of October 1943, told its readers that: *'Berets are "tops" in hat fashions this winter … a beret made in a soft floppy material such as velvet will keep its smart upward thrust if you stitch a circle of milliner's wire into the crown. And did you know that a beret that's been caught out in the rain won't shrink if you dry it with a pudding plate tucked inside it.'*

As well as being colourful and cheap, headscarves were versatile. They could be worn over the shoulders, round the neck, doubled over and draped over the head [this was referred to as 'peasant style'], or as a turban for housework or gardening. The turban effect was achieved by folding the scarf in half, corner-to-corner, to make a triangle, then working from the corner-to-corner base, folding over about 3 inches wide, and repeating until the whole scarf has been folded into a strip – think of rolling it into a tube and then flattening it. Put the centre of the strip at the back of the head, touching the nape of the neck, with the point on the inside, facing down, then bring the two ends round the head and tie in a knot at the front. This kept the hair neatly out of the way. For especially dirty jobs the scarf would only be part rolled, leaving a flap of about a foot, then the scarf would be fitted as before with the flap pointing up, this would be brought over the head, and then the two points tied as before, but over the flap.

With the coming of rationing, large head scarves, over 5¼ sq ft were two coupons, smaller versions, one coupon. Hats were not covered by rationing or price controls. They were, however, subject to controls such as the Limitation of Supply Orders. As such,

prices soared. As the war dragged on, and hats became ever more difficult to get, the head scarf was a ready replacement. Even if you couldn't get a new one: *'You can get several good head scarf squares out of some old patterned evening dresses. All you have to do is to machine around the edges, making a very narrow hem.'* **Woman's Weekly**, of February 1945, came up with a new idea: *'Some of the new ones you see are extraordinarily attractive. A brooch pinned to the centre above the forehead gives a nice touch. (A new place to wear his insignia?)'*

The snood was a kind of loose bag worn over the head, a cross between a hair net and a string bag. They were perfect for keeping the hair in place, without ruining the perm. They were very much a part of the forties look, as **Woman & Home** magazine of November 1942 put it: *'Snoods appear everywhere. They seem to go as well with a fur coat as with the year-before-last tweed.'*

◀ Whilst hats were not rationed, their prices soared, and many found it convenient, or economic, to make their own, like this one from 1942.

▼ A 'Dutch boy' cap, from 1943.

A CROCHETED SNOOD Woman & Home

Materials: A small ball of brightly coloured left-over 3-ply fingering or jumper yarn
a number 2 steel crochet hook
3/4 yard of fine round elastic
3/4 yard of inch-wide ribbon for the bow on top
Begin at the lower edge by working a foundation of 151 ch.
First row: 1 l.tr. in 11th ch. from hook, * 4 ch., miss 4 ch., 1 l.tr. in next ch., making 1 sp.; repeat from * 27 times more, 10 ch., turn.
Second row: 1 l.tr. in first sp., * 4 ch., 1 l.tr., in next sp.; repeat from * to the end, 10 ch., turn.
Repeat the 2nd row 22 times more, making 24 rows altogether. Fasten off.
To gather the snood:
Gather the two sides separately, making one gathering stitch in the side of every row. Draw the sts. closely together and fasten off. Thread the elastic through the holes along the top and bottom, and adjust the length of the elastic to the size of the head. Join the ends by sewing or a small, neat knot.
Tie the ribbon in a bow and sew to the top.

The **Home Companion,** of March 1943, recommended: *'A plain snood can go gay for party occasions if it's decked out with a bunch of flowers across the top. Match the flower colours with your frock and you'll look as gay as gay.'* Snoods also went particularly well with the small trilby-type hat, perched on the front of the head, with the rest of the hair worn long under it.

▸ The snood. An all-purpose piece of headwear – a plain one could be worn for daywear, or a sequined one for a dance, interlaced with small flowers or topped with a small posy for a wedding, worn in bed to cover your curlers, or worn in combination with a hat for going out.

There were seasonal variations. In the summer: *'Generally speaking, straws are worn with light-weight materials, felts and velours with heavy materials. If you are choosing a summer straw to wear with a very dressy, ornamented frock, don't choose one covered with flowers and veiling, or else you'll simply, look overdressed. A fairly plain straw trimmed with ribbon is right. A simple frock that is draped and gathered can take a fussy hat. A tailored linen frock or summer suit should be crowned with a sailor straw or, if you are tall enough, a sombrero.*

'When you are choosing a winter hat look at it in relation to your coat. A brim that dips at the back is no good at all with a high-collared overcoat, as the coat collar will knock it up over your eyes. If you want a hat for a plain, tailored suit, get one with simple lines. A hat with a small brim over the eyes and a turn-up brim at the back is most suitable.' **Sew & Save.**

As with clothes, hat shortages might be answered by making your own. **Home Notes** advised: *'The turban is a straight strip measuring 2 yds by 6 ins.; when finished, run a gathering thread straight across the centre and wind it round with the wool for two or three turns. Catch the two sides together for 9 ins. Slip it over your head bonnet-fashion, cross the ends at the back and bring them round to the top of your head; tie with a half-knot, then twist the remainder of each end over and over the strip, to form a halo. Knit a straight scarf for your throat, 1½ yds. by 8 ins.'*

Home Companion, of March 1943, gave instructions for making a skull cap: *'Piece bag scraps in bright woollen oddments go to make it, and a flat-iron gives the pattern! Lay your iron down on a piece of paper, pencil round the shape, then use the pattern to cut out four neat little gores. When these are seamed together, turn the lower edge in and line your cap with a scrap of silk. With your nearest and dearest's regimental badge pinned to the front of it, that little cap will be smart enough to set at anyone, and as the making time is only half an evening, and the cost nothing, you may like to have more than one. Perhaps a "tweedy" one for everyday, a black woollen one, embroidered with bright wool flowers (gloves to match, please!) with a top-knot of gay Spring flowers! This little bit of nonsense you can keep for the "gay* goings and happy happenings" of hubby's leave, because if a man's seen nothing but the inside of a tank for months, he's going to adore seeing a "fussy" little hat for a change.'

Sew & Save included instructions for a fish-net toque:

'A very pretty toque can be made from 4 yards of coloured fish-net and ¾ yard of buckram. Cut the buckram 4 inches wide, and long enough to fit round your head, then join it up into an upstanding circle, by sewing the two ends together with stab-stitch. Cut off half-a-yard of fish-net to make the crown of your hat, and wind the rest of it round the buckram shape. Leaving a length of about 10 inches to hang loose, start winding over and over the buckram from the back of the shape. Do this fairly tightly so that there are no gaps of buckram showing. When you have covered the shape, fold the fish-net into one-third of its width and wind round a second time so that you get an even, substantial roll all round the shape. The end left over is allowed to hang loose at the back with the end that you left when you started.

'To make the crown, put the half-yard of fish-net loosely over your head, and fit the shape down on to it. When it is comfortable, lift it off carefully, holding the top piece for the crown in place as you do so. Then turn it upside down and carefully pin the crown into the shape all round. Sew down firmly and your toque is finished.'

Alternatively, you could use the crown of an old hat to make a fez, trimmed with thick cord and a tassel. This should be worn with your hair 'halo-wise'. Alternatively, you could tat some rainbow netting in coloured silks, then stitch it over the crown or brim of a navy felt; you could also tat a little extra to cover the collar and cuffs of a navy frock for a complete outfit. Or you could knit a woolly with a matching pixie hood.

One favourite of the time was the 'Dutch cap'. This was a variation on the pixie hood, based on the traditional cap worn by Dutch girls, although confusingly, the term was later used to describe a contraceptive device. The wartime Dutch cap was a fairly simple shape and therefore easy to knit or make from material.

◀ A fez. Many women made their own from the crown of an old hat, and a tassel.

▼ The 'Dutch cap'. The name has changed meaning in the intervening years, but the Dutch cap was originally a variation on the children's 'pixie hood'.

TO RENEW A SHABBY FELT HAT

Take out any lining and remove the ribbon or trimmings. Careful steaming is generally all that is needed to clean it. Put the hat close to the spout of a boiling kettle, keeping it moving and taking care not to saturate it. After this, dry the hat by the fire and when quite dry, brush it. Repeat if necessary. If this doesn't do the trick, you might have a go with ammonia and warm water mixed in equal parts; rub it on very gently with a clean dry cloth, working with the nap of the felt.

If the hat has shrunk or lost its shape, hold it in steam again, your fingers inside the crown, and stretch it round with your hands. When it is back in shape dry it in an oven set low.

Ribbons should be washed in soapy lukewarm water, and rinsed in warm water – you were advised to add a little vinegar. If the ribbon lost its body, the advice was to dissolve a teaspoonful of ordinary gum in a pint of boiling water; then when cool, soak the ribbon in it for a few minutes. Dry it between a soft towel, squeezing out the moisture with your hands, then roll into a tight roll. **Sew & Save** advised that: 'A corded or patterned ribbon is ironed on the wrong side; dark-coloured ribbons should also be ironed on the wrong side. Smooth-faced and pastel-coloured ribbons should be ironed on the right side.' To replace a lost or faded petersham band, the new ribbon should also be steamed, so that, as the crown narrows, the lower edge of the ribbon will be longer than the top edge.

One week after the outbreak of war, the **Daily Mirror** wrote:

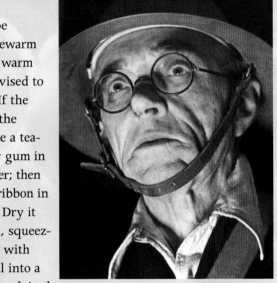

'Envy the ARP men their steel helmets? You needn't. There are plenty in every kitchen. Metal bowls, cullenders, will all give useful protection against flying debris. So, ladies, choose a becoming "tin hat" from the kitchen shelf, line it with some cloth and ... it'll look just like the real thing.'

Well, perhaps not, although they might afford some protection. Early in the blitz, my grandfather, a firewatcher, wore a dustbin lid, tied on with one of my nan's old stockings!

By early 1940 it was possible to buy ladies' hats, 'reinforced with a lightweight steel cap and an anti-concussion bandeau of aerated rubber which affords protection to the sensitive portion of the brain and ear-drums.' These did not catch on.

Helmets could be bought from hatshops. Dunn's sold a Bakelite version. Early in the war, there were a few metal versions available, especially for children, although most were little more than toys and would, in reality, have provided no more protection than their school cap. William Brown, eponymous hero of Richmal Crompton's books, wanted a tin hat: 'Very inferior ones could be bought for as little as sixpence in Hadley, but William did not want an inferior one, and in any case he did not possess sixpence. The one he wanted cost one and six.' **William and the Evacuees**.

Members of ARP, police and the fire service were issued with standard 'tommy' helmets. Later, fire watchers were issued with a different, domed tin helmet, which were also issued to many fire guards. As with Service gas masks, these were often carried when not on duty during periods of raiding. Some private firms produced canvas slings or dual-purpose gas mask/helmet haversacks to help carry them, though most people slung them over their gas mask case.

▾ Advert for a fibre helmet. Besides these civilians could also buy steel and bakelite versions.

GLOVES

'Wear gloves only to keep warm, and when you take them off put them in your pocket or bag. Thousands of gloves are lost every year.' Board of Trade 'Make Do and Mend' booklet.

Gloves containing leather or fur were two coupons. Those without, only one. One tip for refurbishing old leather gloves was to use a good shoe dye on them. Better still to make your own out of scraps, or non-rationed felt. The Board of Trade suggested: *'When men's socks are too worn in the feet for further darning, make them into small-sized gloves or full-sized mittens. Trace your hand on paper, cutting out desired pattern. Place this on sock, using ankle end for wrist, and with thumb protruding over back seam. Thumb is cut separately from best part of instep and inserted into place. Sew with cotton. Scraps left over may be used to reinforce existing socks.'* **101 Ways to Save Money in Wartime** worked on a similar idea: *'Cut off the foot at the instep. Work a row of crochet blanket stitching round the edge, forming a division to separate fingers and thumb.'*

▶ A range of hand-knitted gloves and mittens for adults and children.

BELTS

One simple way of ringing the changes on a frock or skirt was to add a new, colourful, home-made belt. **Everywoman** suggested that: *'A soft chamois leather can be cut into a belt and gilded with paint.'* **Woman's Weekly** advised: *'Scores of brilliantly coloured leather shoelaces attached to the ends of a plain belt – no buckle, just tie the ends loosely in front.'* Or alternatively: *'A wide satin ribbon belt with cross-stitched embroidery in a pattern on the front. Black cross-stitch on an ice-blue ribbon would be effective.'*

Home Companion's idea was to: *'Wear all at once three or four narrow belts, each in a different colour. Fastened one above the other they give great interest in the frock's midriff, and they look beautifully cheerful.'* But it warned: *'This is a notion to be carried out only if you are really slim!'*

'A crocheted belt – made from one ounce of double knitting wool, using a number 11 crochet hook, the medallions measuring 1³⁄₄ inches across.

'To work a medallion – make 6 chain, and slip-stitch to the first stitch to form a ring. 1st round: 3 chain to stand for the first treble, then 14 treble more into the ring. At the end slip-stitch to the top of the 3 chain at the beginning of the round.

'2nd round: 3 chain, 1 treble into the top of the first treble,

taking up both loops at the top of each stitch, then 2 trebles into each stitch all round. Slip-stitch to top of 3 chain at beginning of round and fasten off.

'Make 12 medallions more for a belt measuring about 24 inches long, then sew them together at one side with the same wool.

'With finer wool such as 3-ply fingering, and in a contrasting colour or black, work a length of crochet chain measuring 3 yards long. Fold this in half and 8 inches down from the folded end make a knot with the two thicknesses. Now beginning with the two loose ends of the black chain, begin threading cross-wise through each medallion, leaving 5 trebles free between the two cords. Cross the cords on the face of the medallion and pass down through corresponding spaces between two trebles on the opposite half of the same medallion. Cross the cords again at the back so that a small cross appears at the junction of the two medallions, and bring up each cord in the same position as on the first medallion.

'When the medallions are all threaded leave one inch of the two cords free and knot below that position. Make two small tassels and sew one to each end of the cords.' **Woman & Home.**

Another suggestion was to make a belt from webbing or wide braids to be found in a saddler's shop, which could be bought in plain colours and inch-wide horizontal stripes. You then cut up an old leather belt to make the end fastenings on the new webbing belt.

▸ A belt was one easy way to ring the changes on a tired frock, and there were many instructions for making your own, such as these.

BAGS & BASKETS

A shopping bag, always useful, became a necessity after the 1940 Control of Paper Order directed that: *'No person shall in ... any sale by retail, wrap or pack with paper any article which does not reasonably require such wrapping or packing for its protection.'*

Few families could afford a refrigerator and freezers did not exist, so shopping in the forties was a completely different experience to today's massive monthly boot-load from the supermarket; shopping then was done on a daily basis. True, some goods might be delivered by the shops, but as fuel and manpower shortages hit home, more and more was carried by the housewife in her own shopping bag or basket.

After the introduction of food rationing in January 1940, many off-ration items became increasingly difficult to get, and when they did appear, a queue would soon form. If you saw a queue, you joined it, because at the end of it there was likely to be something well-worth queuing for. For this reason, you needed your shopping bag constantly at hand to put the precious cargo in, be it oranges, stockings or some face powder. In the country, the bag would also be useful for carrying food finds such as wild mushrooms or blackberries.

From November 1941, shopkeepers were not allowed to provide wrapping paper for goods sold. You had to provide your own – even for fish and chips! The shopping bag became even more necessary, and most would now include paper of some sort for wrapping purchases, alongside the family's ration books.

Clutch bags had been very popular in the thirties, and continued to be so in the first half of the war, but by 1942 the far more practical shoulder bag or 'satchel bag' was becoming fashionable. Like everything else, bags became difficult to find, especially in leather, so DIY versions sprang up, made of brightly coloured felt, string, etc.

'Make a pochette in felt to match your dress trimmings, or in a piece of the material left over from your frock. You need only 3/8 of a yard (13 1/2 inches) of 36-inch material. You will also need 3/8 of a yard of buckram. It costs about 1/9 a yard. From these you can make a pochette 12 inches wide and 9 inches deep, large enough to carry make-up, keys, hankie, and the couple of bills or letters that always seem to be in every woman's handbag.

'Cut your buckram into a rectangle 27 inches long by 12 inches wide. Then lay it on a flat surface over your length of material, which should be cut 28 inches long by 13 inches wide. The extra inch of material is used for 1/2 inch turnings all round. Turn the material in and tack it evenly all round the edges of the buckram,

▼ A clutch bag, home-made from knotted string.

as close in as you can. Be careful to keep it well and evenly stretched across the buckram, and don't let the tacking stitches come through again on to the material. Still keeping the whole thing laid out flat, cut a lining from 3/8 of a yard of dark sateen or from any odd dark pieces you may have in your piece-bag.

'The lining should be turned under all round and hemmed, pressed on the wrong side, laid over the buckram and over the tacked edges of the material, and lightly pinned into place. Join it carefully to the edges of the material that are overlapping the buckram, to cover the tacks, and stitch with invisible slipstitches.

'Now fold the whole thing into three equal parts, each 9 inches deep, The first two sections make the bag, the top one is the overlap. The sides are joined on the outside with close, tight, small oversewing stitches in the same coloured thread as the material, so that they do not show. Sew on a couple of press-studs just inside the two top corners of the overlap. Mark the points of these with chalk and press down on to the body of the bag, so that you have the exact position on which to sew the other halves of the studs. **Sew & Save.**

Powder compacts, or flapjacks, were almost compulsory. They came in a wide range of shapes (circular or square being the most

common), materials (plastic and metal), colours, designs and sizes. Early in the war, 'sweetheart' designs were common, bearing the insignia of a loved one's military unit. Civilian variations with ARP or AFS badges were also available.

Like everything else, they became scarce and had to be made to last. In January 1945, **Woman's Weekly** told its readers how to make a new puff for their compact: 'You can make a pretty one if you have a skein of pale blue or pink embroidery wool to spare. Cut the double skein into four, 2½ inch lengths. Place one on top of the other and with a thread of wool, wind tightly round the centre of them, about six times and knot securely. Then, with a large needle, fluff out the ends all round to make a ball shape. When this is done, trim the ends with a pair of scissors. Finish with a bow at the back.'

The **Home Companion** had this advice on mending the sifter in a compact: 'You know how maddening it is when the muslin wears out – you spill your precious powder everywhere, and all the time get too much of it on your puff. The way out of that spot of bother is to make a new sifter for your-self using a snippet of an old silk stocking for the job.

'What you'll need to do first is to cut away the worn muslin from your sifter. Now brush the edges of the sifter frame lightly with gum, slip the frame into the stocking, pull an unladdered part of the stocking tightly over it and let it stick. When it's dry cut the sifter out of the stocking, leaving a turning all the way round. Gum this down and the job's done, and most professional it looks. Be sure and hunt up one of your old pure silk stockings for this mend won't you? And, of course, wash it first!'

Lipstick cases used scarce raw materials such as metal and, by 1943, if you could get lipstick at all, it was probably in refill form. In February 1944 **Good Housekeeping** reported: 'you have a choice of the new wooden Utility lipstick case, which is very popular, or a gilt metal one with a favourite lipstick ... the range of shades is limited.'

Early in the war the use of match cases was common. These were a metal box which fitted round a match box, leaving uncovered the ends and one of the striking sides. The case was usually covered in a plasticised

◂ A hand-knitted clutch bag. Initials were a popular form of decoration.

paper, bearing a design, Again, regimental badges were given as sweetheart tokens; there were also the usual civilian versions.

Wood shortages soon meant a corresponding shortage of matches – 'Use matches sparingly' wartime boxes proclaim. Demand for petrol lighters surged, but like everything else, their manufacture was strictly controlled. Do-it-yourself versions became common, factory workers used what was available to produce fairly crude models; a large hexagonal nut shaved down with a penny each side made up the body of one common model, 'trench-art' type versions made from a bullet case, were also common. At the end of 1941, various Utility designs, made mainly of plastic and using little metal, were sold at a controlled price of 6s 6d; at the same time the government decreed that no other lighters could be manufactured commercially.

'Supplies are plentiful, and the Utility lighter, though inferior to the typical automatic lighter of pre-war days, is a neat, well-designed substitute which, partly because of the acute shortage of matches, is widely popular.' **Civilian Supplies in Wartime Britain.**

Also inside the handbag would be a purse, often matching, and a growing number of personal papers; ration books were nearly always carried just in case something special turned up in the shops. Apart from ration books for food, points, personal points and clothing, there might also be petrol, kerosene, poultry feed, livestock feed, pigeon feed or furniture ration books. There would also be identity cards (never ID cards!) – green for adult (after 1943), brown for children, or service identity cards for Home Guardsmen, ARP workers, Fire Guards, AFS and other services.

UMBRELLAS & SUITCASES

The umbrella, long the symbol of the well-dressed British male, substantially disappeared along with much else due to the shortage of raw materials, as did the suitcase; typically made of leather or pig-skin in the thirties, by the end of the war available only in fibre or cardboard.

Umbrellas were not rationed. Men's umbrellas were, as today, black with walking-stick type handles, while women's umbrellas came in a range of colours. As with much else unrationed, they became hard to get, and were often patched or mended.

Most pre-war suitcases were of leather, but these soon became unobtainable – in 1941, the supply of suitcases was cut by two-thirds – and Utility fibre versions took their place. Old cases were renovated; advice was to dust it, then give it a good wash with warm soapy water to remove any dirt and grease. Leave it to dry out completely, then give it a good polish with furniture cream. If the leather has worn away at the corners or edges get a small bottle of leather dye the same colour as the case and apply thinly and evenly with a small piece of sponge over the rubbed places. Leave to dry, then polish.

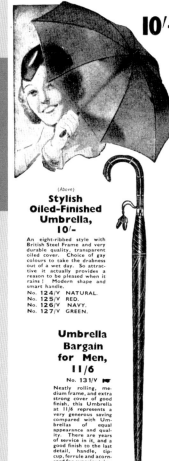

10/-

(Above)
Stylish Oiled-Finished Umbrella, 10/-

An eight-ribbed style with British Steel Frame and very durable quality, transparent oiled cover. Choice of gay colours to take the drabness out of a wet day. So attractive it actually provides a reason to be pleased when it rains! Modern shape and smart handle.

No. 124/V NATURAL.
No. 125/V RED.
No. 126/V NAVY.
No. 127/V GREEN.

Umbrella Bargain for Men, 11/6

No. 131/V ☞
Neatly rolling, medium frame, and extra strong cover of good finish, this Umbrella at 11/6 represents a very generous saving compared with Umbrellas of equal appearance and quality. There are years of service in it, and a good finish to the last detail, handle, tipcup, ferrule and acorncord for superior trimming. Plain BLACK cover.

11/6

TORCHES & GAS MASKS

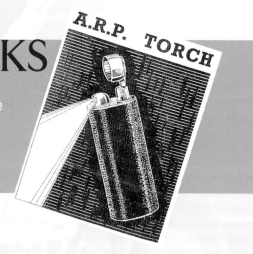

A.R.P. TORCH

'Yes, Dear, we got on all right in the Blackout, but he had to put three layers of tissue paper over his torch!' Punchline from one of many saucy postcards of the period inspired by the blackout.

The Blackout led to numerous accidents in the darkened streets, creating a huge demand for pocket torches. At first they were banned, but from September 13, 1939, due to widespread public protests, it became permissible to use a small pocket torch in the street, as long as it was pointed downwards and was put out when the air-raid warning was sounded. Home Office regulations stated that the light could not be more than one candle power; this was usually achieved by the glass being masked by two thicknesses of tissue paper. A scene from the 1944 film, **A Canterbury Tale**, shows a newly-arrived US serviceman mocking the low level of light from his

▸ Advert for gas mask bags. The masks were issued in a cardboard box, and manufacturers were quick to offer a range of carriers.

Smart Gas Mask Container-Handbag with Purse to match

Very large and roomy design specially shaped for extra width in base to take gas mask, with plenty of room to spare for toilet requisites, etc. Made in good wearing Morocco Grain with stylish loop handle. Nicely lined. APPROX. SIZE: 6 x 9 ins. BLACK only. No. **176/V**

8/-

British companions' torches. 'I'll show you a real flashlight' he says, producing a dazzling beam, which immediately brings a cry of 'Put that light out!'. Most torches were of the small, cylindrical pattern, and used the famous – or infamous – number 8 battery, one of the earliest shortage items.

At the time of the Munich Crisis in September 1938, most people in this country had been issued with gas masks by the local ARP. These were not collected back in afterwards, so in September 1939, the vast majority of people had them ready when war was declared. There were three types of gas mask, more properly termed respirators, carried by adult civilians. By far the most common was

the civilian gas mask. This had a soft rubber face piece and a wide single eyepiece. Members of the ARP, such as wardens, were issued with the Civilian Duty mask. This was far more robust than the ordinary civilian mask and had a large filter on the front, and two separate circular eye pieces. The third was the Service mask, which had a corrugated tube coming from the front of the mask, going into a filter carried in a haversack round the neck; these were issued to members of the Services, the police, firemen, some members of the ARP, such as rescue workers, and, later, the Home Guard.

Although you were not supposed to carry either the Service or Civilian Duty masks

▼ A children's march from early in the war encouraging people to carry their gas masks. (Courtesy Kent Messenger)

when not on duty, carrying instead your issue civilian mask, photographs show that this rule was often broken. Civilian Duty masks were carried in a variety of carriers, but by far the most common was a loose canvas or hessian bag, usually in light brown, on an inch-wide white strap. The bag being secured by a draw-string round the top, or by a buttoned-down flap. The Service mask was almost always carried in its bag of issue, being a more rigid, roughly square bag in brown or green canvas, with a 2-inch wide strap.

The far more common civilian mask was issued in a cardboard box, through which a string could be threaded for carrying purposes, but the boxes were far from robust or weather-proof. As soon as war was declared, commercially made gas mask cases of various descriptions and price were on sale everywhere.

The simplest, DIY version was to cover your cardboard box with some sort of waterproof material, such as 'American cloth' or gabardine. The cheapest commercial cases extended this idea, being a soft fabric case into which the gas mask, complete with its cardboard box, was placed. There were numerous other versions, metal cylinders or boxes, and hand-bag versions in such mater-

ials as canvas, gabardine, Rexine, and leather. In May, 1940, rumours were circulating of a new gas, 'arsine', against which the existing mask was ineffective. Over the next two months the ARP fitted everyone's mask with an additional 'contex' filter, fastened on to the end of the existing filter with adhesive tape. This made the mask longer and meant that some unofficial containers became difficult, or downright impossible to close.

'There is no obligation to carry them about and nobody can be fined for not doing so. The Government, however, advises that they should be carried in neutral and evacuation areas.' **The War Time Lawyer,** 1940. However, when after the first few days of the war the complete ban on public entertainments was lifted, customers were often only allowed into cinemas and dance-halls if they were carrying their gas masks. As the Phoney War dragged on, these restrictions were dropped and it became increasingly rare for people to carry gas masks, and not all the gas mask cases on view actually had a mask inside. One correspondent wrote to the **Daily Mirror** of an elderly lady she had met: *'She opened her box and to my surprise it contained half a dozen eggs.'*

As early as October 1939 the government had announced that it was not necessary to carry your respirator at all times in reception areas, although they still worked hard to encourage people to carry them in danger areas; poster campaigns warned: *'The enemy will give no warning – carry your gas mask everywhere'.* However, events finally settled the issue in the latter half of 1942, when in order to conserve rubber, the government relaxed its calls for everyone to carry their gas masks during the day, even in danger areas. It was bowing to the inevitable. That year, in the comedy film, **The Goose Steps Out**, starring Will Hay, a trainee German spy is told that to appear English he must be sure not to carry his gas mask.

▾ One of the many cheap gas mask cases on sale in the autumn of 1939.

SPECTACLES

'"Jim Crow" Spectacles are scientifically designed to assist in the responsible duty of "spotting" and identifying aircraft. Spotters wearing these spectacles can look direct into the sun without discomfort. An essential part of every spotter's equipment —retail price 15/-' Advert for Perimet spectacles, December 1940.

◄ Examples of glasses from 1939 to 1940.

One of the biggest concerns regarding gas masks was the wearing of spectacles. For the more robust Civilian Duty and Service masks, the Mark III respirator glasses had been designed; these had hyper-thin, flexible arms, which would be sandwiched against the head by the respirator, thus keeping the whole thing air-tight. These did not work with the normal, far thinner, civilian respirator. Many private firms issued gas mask spectacles, usually held on with a band of elastic which passed round the head, or over the ears and under the chin. The government however, steadfastly refused to authorise any of them, arguing that the elastic would form a furrow in the skin, allowing the gas to enter the mask, or the front of the spectacles would distort the front of the mask, with the same effect, or that they would rub against the soft rubber of the mask, weakening and eventually puncturing it.

A debate sprang up in the pages of **The Optician** about the suitability of various gas mask spectacles, including a popular suggestion that lorgnettes were the perfect solution; the eventual outcome was advice that those who could not do without their glasses should buy a Civilian Duty mask (16/6) and Mark IIIs from their opticians.

There was another noteworthy wartime innovation in spectacles. In October 1939 Levers advertised 'Luminite' spectacles 'to prevent blackout accidents'. These were 'treated with a high-grade Radio-active luminous material' which caused 'the front of the frame to glow intensely in the dark without discomfort to the wearer' so that 'the wearer's presence is therefore obvious even at a considerable distance during the black-out.' These do not seem to have caught on.

In terms of ordinary spectacles, there were many different types to be had, including plastic frames in a range of colours;

◄ Advertisment for gas mask glasses from 1939.

▸ Examples of glasses and sun glasses from 1939 and 1940.

in May 1940 one firm offered women's frames in shell, flesh, daylight blue, crystal and pearl. There were also metal frames, mostly 9 ct. gold, rolled gold, or nickel, some with imitation tortoiseshell covering, as well as real tortoiseshell frames, and even rimless glasses. Men's plastic frames were usually in black, or light or dark tortoiseshell. Shapes varied from round through oval to nearly rectangular and octagonal, and lenses included bi-focals.

Women were concerned about glasses ruining their looks. The **Home Companion**, of April 1943, advised: *'The main thing to remember with glasses is that you've got to keep all the features clear and well defined, otherwise you get that cluttered-up look. Eyebrows should be neat and tidy; lipstick firmly applied to give your mouth a clean, firm line; be careful to work your rouge well in so that it looks as natural as possible; if possible, do your hair away from your face, so that there are no stray ends or loose curls to spoil the outline. Anything fussy in the way of a hairdo isn't for those of us who wear glasses.'*

Sun glasses, or sun goggles, as they were commonly called, were widely used, from the extremely cheap – all in one piece – to those supplied by opticians. Surprisingly, those available included Ray-Bans and Polaroids. If you normally wore glasses you were most likely to wear either 'fitovers' which clipped onto your existing glasses, or your normal glasses with a larger pair of sun glasses over the top.

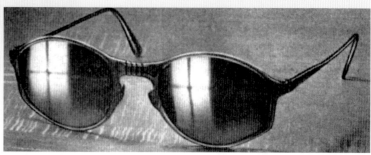

JEWELLERY & WATCHES

'Owing to the great shortage of watches, we are prepared to purchase any second-hand watches you may have in reasonable condition.'
Advertisement in the Bognor Regis Post June 1944.

At first, the most popular form of wartime jewellery was the sweetheart brooch – the regimental badge of a loved one, often in metal, sometimes enamelled, on a mother-of-pearl background. These were usually in the form of brooches, although rings, ear-rings and scarf-pins were also available. There were ATS, WAAF and WRNS versions too. For those who could afford it there were regimental badges set with marcasites, and even precious metals set with gem-stones. Soon, however, the use of scarce materials for jewellery was legislated against. The Limitation of Supplies Orders which set strict limits on the amounts of consumer goods which a manufacturer could purchase were succeeded by the Control of Manufacture and Supply Orders. These covered most items (other than clothing, which had Orders all its own), prohibiting the manufacture of all but the most necessary articles. In the area of jewellery, only identification bracelets, cuff-links, studs and wedding rings were allowed to be manufactured, and then only under licence. Later, there were plain 9 ct. gold Utility wedding rings, although these were never produced in enough volume to meet demand.

Jewellers could still sell second-hand jewellery and the newspapers were full of advertisements offering good prices for old baubles. In February 1942, **Woman and Home** reported that: *'The jewellers' shops say they could sell every locket they put in the window over and over again. Anything sentimental in the way of jewellery is bought as soon as it gets into the shop, whether it's a true-love knot, a locket, or keepsake ring with clasped hands. Even charms take second place to these true-heart ornaments.'*

As with clothes, those who had enough money usually had pre-war jewellery to fall back on. The **Tatler** of August 1942 described: *'… Lady Dalrymple Champneys, in white, with touches of black, and with the most lovely huge diamond brooch on her shoulder; Sylvia Lady Poulett, also wearing a lovely brooch, hers a very large one, too, made of sapphires bordered with diamonds, beautifully designed…'*

With the lack of jewellery in the shops, do-it-yourself versions became all the rage. Magazines came out with ever-more inventive ideas for using unlikely materials to make your own, such as old silver cutlery to make brooches and necklaces.

▲ Ciro ad from 1940 showing some of the styles popular at the time. Note the 'badge brooches', otherwise known as sweetheart brooches.

Factories were a great source of raw materials, and many workers used scraps to produce all sorts of bits and bobs in their spare time. Perspex was popular, as were lengths of fine insulated wire and coins. Often the finished articles would be traded outside the factories. Small Spitfire brooches were popular early on, and later, Victory 'Vs', in a wide range of materials.

Even before the war, buttonholes were a popular way of cheering up a woman's suit or dress which had been worn to boredom. **The Lady's Companion**, of March 1940 (before most shortages

▸ Home-made but-tonholes were made from a wide range of materials, including felt, as with these examples.

were really biting) advised its readers: *'The latest but-tonhole posies are made of coloured cellophane, and very cheery they are. You could easily make your own. Other ideas you could copy are buttonholes made of coloured beech nuts and suede flowers, wool flowers, raffia, oiled silk, or felt.'*

Here are a few examples of the creativity and the range of materials used by various magazines for DIY buttonholes and other jewellery throughout the war. They were such a common sight that they will add authenticity and interest to any forties' outfit.

> **With the lack of jewellery in the shops, do-it-yourself versions became all the rage**

'Tie a gay ribbon on the old key-ring [not the ring itself – the pierced disc on which an address might be engraved], *add a safety pin at the knot, paint the disc to match the ribbon and add a bold, black initial. Worn in the buttonhole it will provide a new uplift to an old suit.'* **Woman & Home,** November 1942.

'A pretty ornament to decorate the lapel of your suit or to wear on a pocket can be made so easily from a few beads from some broken necklaces. In the little sketch on this page you see a sweet fob I made and attached to a big velvet bow.

'It is very easy to make yourself one of these fobs. First thread your beads on to some strong thread, or even fine wire, securing the lowest bead firmly with a knot or a double twist. Then attach your strings of beads to a small safety-pin and stitch your bow to the top of the pin.' **Mother,** May 1944.

Another idea was to use acorns, with a little twig attached. Remove the nuts and let the cups dry, then enamel them inside and out with bright colours, and when dry, bunch them together attractively. You could use rose hips which had been hollowed out to make a necklace, and when dry, varnished and threaded bead fashion on some coloured string. Another idea for making necklaces was to use chicken rings (from a bird shop), in different colours.

You could even turn your hand to making cuff links to match a shirt; use a tiny piece from the shirt tail and use it to cover four smallish linen buttons. Finish off neatly and link them together in pairs with a short length of cotton strands neatly button-holed over.

Attractive old buttons which had a shank at the back, could be converted into brooches by sewing one on to a small piece of felt and sewing a safety pin onto the other side. Smaller buttons became the centre pieces of brooches, often built around a curtain ring, covered with wire or wool, and fastened with a safety pin, or an old-fashioned, man's collar pin. Other versions were made of carved wood or plastic, sewn from felt, usually in the shape of flowers, or made from metal.

A Heart Buttonhole

Cut out four little hearts from [red] felt. Lay two together, stuff with cotton wool and oversew together with black cotton. Make a bow of scarlet ribbon, attach one heart to each end and sew the bow to a tie pin. [or safety pin]. Woman, October 1940.

Another idea was to make clay beads from Pyruma [fireclay]. Roll a piece roughly the size of the required bead into a ball between the palms of your hands. Using a metal skewer or knitting-needle pierce it through the centre and then roll it lightly along the outside of the palm of one hand, into the barrel shape. Place it hole upwards on to a tin tray. Make a total of six barrel-shaped beads and one small round ball for a fastener. Then put the tin on top of the rack over the gas stove and leave it there for several days or you could pop it into a hot oven for about thirty minutes on baking-day. When the beads are quite dry and hard paint them.

Badges were a common sight worn by men and children, especially. There were two main types of wartime badge worn by civilians: the civilian service identity badge and the war charity badge.

Civilian service badges started to be used in the first World War, when badges proclaiming 'on war service' were issued to munitions and other war-workers to stave off criticism from those who thought any man not in military uniform was a coward. Early in the Second World War, the Merchant Navy suffered huge losses in the Atlantic, while the home population grumbled about the boredom of the Phoney War. Members of the Merchant Navy had no uniform to mark them out, and a lapel badge was struck for them. Other lapel badges

included the ARP, not issued with uniform until late 1940, the Observer Corps (later the Royal Observer Corps), the WVS, the Home Guard, off-duty AFS, fire watchers, railway-men, and knitters for the Merchant Navy and other comforts funds.

Some, such as the silver (later white metal) ARP badge, were issued by the service. Company identity badges, such as that of the BBC, were issued by the employer, while

A BUTTONHOLE MADE FROM A FIR CONE

'Besides a small fir cone, you will need a piece of green leather or felt cut [into a leaf shape]; and 3/4 yard of brown or green leather thonging for the stems (or cord could be used instead).

'Cut off the top end of the fir cone, and the piece left will look like an open flower. Paint the outer petals red, or a bright colour to match your scarf, and the centre of the cone pale green or yellow. Use enamel if available. Then leave the flower to dry.

'Cut the thonging into three for the stems. Then knot each piece three or four times at one end. Sew the flower cone firmly to the middle of the stems with the knotted ends hanging. The sewing can be done by winding the cotton in and out of the lower scales of the cone, at the back, so that it does not show.

'Then sew the stems in the centre of the large leather leaf. Finally add a safety pin at the back, for fastening.' *Woman's Weekly*, January 1945.

BESTWAY LEAFLET 686 3d

BUTTONHOLES and NECKLACES
Made in Felt

(Photo : Gaumont British - Gainsborough Star)

Phyllis Calvert

WOMAN AND HOME GAVE INSTRUCTIONS FOR A NECKLET MADE OUT OF WOOL

Cut open a skein of embroidery wool and mark the centre. Remove four strands. Take one of them and twist the middle of it three times round the skein 3/8 of an inch from the centre, then knot firmly. Thread the two ends into a needle and carry them through the skein to the other side of the centre, here twist the wool round three times again in opposite directions, and knot it, thus making the centre bead. Make the other beads similarly, graduating them, using a new strand as required.

To graduate the beads, cut out a few strands of wool from the middle of the skein to thin it for the smaller beads. Wind wool firmly round the necklace ends and fit caps over them. To make a cap, wind wool round the top of the little finger, then darn upwards and downwards, weaving through the threads, and catching the top thread each time. Remove the cap from the finger and stitch it over one end of the necklace. Add half a snap fastener to each end.'

Home-made wartime jewellery, showing just some of the many types of materials used to create the whole range of jewellery – wood, wire, plastic and felt.

▼ Just a few examples of the many lapel badges worn by various civilian groups during the war, including collection badges for war weapons weeks, Spitfire funds, etc.

The 1940s Look

many others were private purchase items, sold by commercial badge makers.

Pre-war versions, such as the ARP badge, and the Civil Nursing Reserve badge, might be in silver; early wartime versions were in chrome, brass, or were enamelled. Later versions became cheaper. Good examples are Women's Land Army, and 'WVS for Civil Defence' badges, early versions of which are enamelled, while later versions look the

same, but the colour is picked out in paint. By mid-wartime many badges, where they continued to be issued, were in plastic.

The other common type was the war-collection badge: the Spitfire Fund badge, War Weapons Weeks, Salute the Soldier Weeks, the Red Cross Penny-a-week club, National Savings and others sold to raise money for war-related causes. These were usually pin-back badges.

No. 920. Gents' fully guaranteed Accurist, bench tested, 15-jewelled Swiss lever movement in 9 ct. solid gold tonneau shaped case, seconds hand, clear bold figures, best quality leather strap.
£17.10.0 post free

No. 843. Gents' fully guaranteed Accurist, 15-jewelled, bench tested, Swiss lever movement, handsome modern 9 ct. gold case, seconds hand, best quality leather strap.
£25.15.0 post free

No. 416. Gents' fully guaranteed Accurist, 15-jewelled, bench-tested, Swiss lever movement in handsome 9 ct. solid gold case ; best quality leather strap.
£16.5.0 post free

★ Five years' written guarantee with each of these watches

Whilst men's pocket watches were still used, wrist watches had become far more fashionable. Their cases came in a range of metals: platinum, 9ct. gold, solid or plated, rolled gold, chrome plated, or in what was described as the latest fashionable material, stainless steel. Many had a small, separate, 'second' dial, usually centre-bottom, although there were some very modern looking 'chronometers' on the market with two and even three small dials. Most modern of all was the 'self-winding' wristwatch, by Messrs W.J. Huber Ltd. 'being actuated by the normal movement of the wrist'. With the advent of the blackout,

luminous dials, usually offered as an optional extra, became very fashionable.

Both men's and women's wrist watches were produced in a wide range of shapes, the most common being round, square, rectangular, and hexagonal.

Women's everyday 'wristlet' watches were usually smaller versions of those worn by men, though dress versions often had marcasites or real stones set into their cases. Also available were pendant watches, as worn by nurses today, although at the time these were worn, often heavily encrusted with stones, as part of evening dress. If your purse did not run to both a wristlet and a pendant watch, you could buy a Vesta watch fob, comprising of a brooch-hanger and fob, 'easily attached and detached, converting a wristlet watch into an attractive fob'. There were even ring-watches.

Watch straps came in a similarly wide range of styles and materials. Popular was the metal expanding bracelet, such as the 'Britannic' comprising of three or five rows of sprung links, in 'gold, silver or platinum'. Other metal straps came in chrome and stainless steel. Most common of all was leather, especially after the Limitation of Supply (Miscellaneous) Order, 1940, cut by three-quarters the production of metal wrist watch straps and watch chains. Robert Pringle and Sons offered men's watchstraps in 'real Morocco, English calf and pigskin leathers, also real Lizard or Crocodile skins. Widths 1/2" to 7/8" ', buckles were typically gilt or EPNS. Women's straps also came in silk or elastic cord, plaited leather and moiré.

With the outbreak of war there was a surge in the sale of identity discs and straps. Responding to this, Denco produced plates which slipped over a watch strap, 'engraved and enamelled with your name and address'. Men's versions came in silver (15/-), and gold (2 guineas), while women's versions came in silver (30/-), silver gilt (37/6), or 9ct. gold (5 guineas).

◄ Accurist wristwatch adverts from 1942 (below) and 1943 (above). Prices rose steeply during the war; the cheapest 1942 model is the equivalent of about £150 today, while the cheapest 1943 version about £400.

WOMEN'S HAIR

'A permanent wave is a necessity for women who are doing war work unless their hair is naturally curly. The demand for Eugene waves has, naturally, greatly increased this year.'
Advert for Eugene waves, December 1941.

Even before clothes rationing was introduced in June 1941, the shortage of clothes in the shops meant that, for most women, a new outfit was not a viable proposition. But you could cheer yourself up with a new hairstyle, from the hairdresser, if you could afford it, or by doing it yourself.

All the new pressures of the war – the blackout, nights spent in the shelter, queuing, Digging for Victory, make do and mending, etc., left little time for personal grooming. In September 1943, **Home Companion** advised

its readers: *'Whatever else you do, keep your hair looking nice. I know it's a bit of a nuisance at times – especially at nights, before you go to bed, and you feel you just can't be bothered to give it those hundred strokes but time spent on your hair is never time wasted. Men notice nice hair even before a pretty face, I believe, and it isn't necessary to have expensive perms and sets in order to make your hair your crowning glory. Just brush it, and then, when you've finished, brush it again.'*

Many of the everyday tasks a woman had to carry out were detrimental to good grooming. **Good Housekeeping** told its readers: *'A bout of cooking often spells ruin to an attractive hairdo, unless you decide to use the steam as an ally by carefully pinning your curls and tying them up in a scarf.'*

From February 1942, even shampoo joined the ever-growing list of hard-to-get products. Soap was the obvious alternative, but you had to do several lathers and rinses. There was a special shredded soap, made for using as shampoo; it had to be added to hot water, then the two boiled until they became a thick liquid. At this point you could add some form of scent – perfume, or more likely, lemon verbena, or the essence of some other scented herb. If you could get hold of shampoo it had to be made to last. In October 1942, **Drene shampoo** advised: *'Put a little more than a teaspoonful of Drene in a breakfast cup – half fill the cup with warm water.'* Then after thoroughly wetting the hair, half the cupful was used, the hair well rinsed, then the process repeated. As a special rinse, vinegar was recommended for dark hair and strained lemon

◄ The blonde look was just as popular in 1940 as it is today. And for many the look came out of a bottle.

juice for fair hair. You didn't have to stick to shampoo, or even soap. For oily hair, advice was to cleanse with starch once a week, while for dandruff, a pre-shampoo rinse with ordinary antiseptic or a teaspoonful of borax in a cup of warm water was recommended.

Even before shortages, people washed their hair far less often than we do today. In December 1939, **Woman's Own** advised: *'Shampoo your hair every other week, and do the job thoroughly.'* **Modern Woman** suggested: *'All your hair wants to look lovely, whatever your age or kind of life, is regular exercise, frequent washing and an occasional meal.'* And what did frequent washing mean? *'Oily hair needs washing once a week, so does hair exposed to much dust in offices and factories. Normal hair, if you live at home, needs washing once every ten days; and dry hair, if not exposed to dusty air, can be washed once a fortnight.'* One letter to **Woman's Weekly** complained that, after its fortnightly wash, the writer's hair became frizzy for several days – was she washing it too often?

Modern Woman recommended massage: *'An oil scalp massage, the oil left on all night, can convert dull, perm-dried hair into soft silky stuff in the most miraculous way. All you need is half an eggcupful of olive oil, almond oil or vegetable oil. Many hairdressers recommend castor oil for the hair. If you wash your hair at home, oil the scalp overnight, if possible. (Tie it up in a scarf to save the pillow case and your feelings when you look in the glass.) For the washing use either a favourite shampoo powder, green soft soap or shredded Castile soap reduced to a jelly by melting in very hot water. Use soft water if possible; if not, fairly hot water is needed for each of the two washes necessary. Lather the soap thoroughly by vigorous massage with the hands, working from the hairline inwards. Then rinse. Lather again with fresh clean water and massage with energy. Unlathered soap is impossible to rinse from the hair. You will need three lots of clean water at least to rinse the hair finally, and the last but one, if the water is hard, should have a tablespoonful or two of vinegar in it.'*

The next part of the ritual that was hair care in the 1940s was setting. Many did this themselves: *'Squeeze the water out of your hair,*

rub it a little with a towel … If your hair is not "easy" hair, inclined to wave or curl, you have probably chosen a very simple style for it. If not, and a few curls are necessary for your type of face, a bottle of setting lotion is worthwhile. If your curls "stay put" easily, a light lotion will be all that you'll need. If it's more difficult, choose one of the more "sticky" ones.

'Don't attempt anything elaborate. Concentrate on a becoming line round the face, comb the longer hair back and set as near the heart's desire as you can manage. You can do things later with those little metal or "pipe cleaner" curlers after the hair is dry. But the front and side hairlines need careful shaping from the start.

'Spray the hair while it is still wet, part it carefully, comb back from the parting, then forward, then back again, until you get the "feel" of the hair.

'Keep the wave positions firm with the left hand as you work with the right, then slip in setting combs into the waves. Curl the ends in little flat snails and hold with two invisible pins. Put on a net and fan dry in a warm room near a fire.' **Modern Woman**, February 1941.

'Tie a net over the top, and don't take that net off until the hair is dry. And, when I say dry, I mean bone dry right through. No hairdresser would touch it till it was dry, and you can't expect to work miracles when you are not a hairdresser.' **Woman's Own**, December 1939.

If you could afford it, you would go to the hairdresser for a shampoo and set but even then, you couldn't relax. *'If you've chosen your hairdresser with care he, or she, will look after your hair's good looks for you. But be firm about wholesome types of soaps and ask for the new oily and conditioning shampoos now available, if your hair is in a poor state of health.'*

'Insist on the line of setting you know becomes you. Left to themselves, some hairdressers treat your head rather as a chef treats an elaborate galantine or "novelty" sweet for an aldermen's banquet. You emerge a mass of perfect but meaningless squirls and curls and squiggles, horrifying to the eye. These hairdressers call themselves stylists and are very important people. They need treating with tact – and firmness.' **Modern Woman.**

CAMILATONE
vitamin shampoo &
TŌNRINZ
toning rinse

..made
all
the
difference

Whatever the colour of your hair there's a **Camilatone** Vitamin Shampoo with a **Tōnrinz** beautifying rinse specially *made for you*. Be sure that the packet you purchase contains the **Tōnrinz** to match your hair.

Golden Brown for Brunettes.
Blonde for the Warm Blonde.
Auburn for all dark and medium shades.
Golden Rinse for all dull and slightly greying hair and for fair shades in general.
White Camilatone (with Blue Rinse) is specially made for grey and silver white hair.

Shampoo and Tōnrinz complete, 6d.
Tōnrinz or Golden Rinse,
separately, 2d.

The perm – permanent wave – had been popular for over thirty years by 1939 and by then it was the very core of women's hairstyles. Everyone who could afford to got a 'perm'. Its bubbly, curly style became the target of those who, on the outbreak of war, wanted everyone to act with restraint:

'*...for goodness sake don't take any notice if long faces are pulled when you announce that you are going to have a perm, or some such so-called luxury – if you've saved up the money for it, have it, and if you've only partially saved have the side pieces done and roll up the back with grips. For half a perm is better than straight bits with curlers in an air raid.*' **Woman and Home.**

A perm was expensive but it lasted a long time, as this letter to **Woman's Weekly** in February 1945 shows: '*It is nearly six months since I had my last permanent wave. Would it be safe for me to have a new one as I still have a little of the previous permanent wave left? – Yes, but be sure that the hairdresser cuts away the remains of the old permanent wave beforehand.*'

Furthermore: '*Hair that has been permanently waved stands up to vigorous brushing just as good-temperedly as naturally curly hair. If it tends to stand on end after being brushed, sprinkle on a few drops of setting lotion, and push the waves in place with your fingers. To hold the waves in place, wear a hair net overnight.*' **Woman's Weekly**, November 1944.

Wearing a hair net at night was not exactly glamorous, nor was it compulsory:

◄ The elaborate permed curls and waves popular in the first years of the war are clearly shown in this ad from 1940.

◄ The perm – as by Eugene, were so well known for the 'Eugene wave', that their adverts, such as this, contained just one word.

'*A few clips or pins under a pretty snood or turban will keep your hair in place, or, if you must wear a net, wear it well back on the head and add a bow of ribbon.*' **Good Housekeeping**, October 1944.

Having a perm took a long time and needed electricity – a service which became far less reliable with the onset of raiding by the Luftwaffe. Many a woman found her styling interrupted by the warning's summons to the shelter. Here the operation might continue, especially if the hairdresser had gone over, as many did, to a non-electric perm.

There were problems once the perm started to work its way out, but **Home Companion** was at hand with the solution: '*My perm's practically out, but I can't have a new one for about two months. Can you suggest any neat way of doing my hair during this time? – All you need is a piece of ribbon about an inch wide. This you tie round your head finishing it in a bow above the forehead. Then tuck all the ends of your hair round and under the ribbon, giving a sort of halo effect. For special occasions when you want to look pretty for your husband home on leave, tuck a small posy of flowers into the ribbon in front.*' Alternatives to a ribbon were an old stocking tied around, or the top of a stocking, cut off, which made an excellent hair band.

Not everyone went to the hairdressers for a perm. There were proprietary home-perm outfits. Norman Longmate records one Timber Corps member paying 14/6 for an Endura home -perm: '*The waving liquid smelt like rotten eggs. It gave, she recalls, a good curl but even though she was working in the open air it took a week to get rid of the smell.*'

Looks were important for the country's morale but there were certain practical considerations to be taken into account. The **Daily Mirror** of September 1939 announced that: '*Hairdressers in the West End of London report the latest coiffeur – the Gas Mask Curl. Idea is to leave centre-parting for the main strap. Clusters of curls stand on either side.*'

At the beginning of the war, shorter hair styles became more popular as women entered the services, where the rule that hair should not touch the back of the collar was strictly enforced. **Home Notes** in December, 1939 reported that: '*Short hair is very fashionable just now: either you can have a smartly-shingled back with your side pieces swept up into combs and flat curls on the top of your head, or you can have your hair cut short all over your head and worn in a mass of soft curls; very youthful and no trouble to keep nice.*'

▼ Even when hair became shorter, an elaborate quiff might still be part of the style, as seen here.

▼ The perm was central to women's hairstyles, but disruption of electricity by raiding meant the machineless perm, as advertised here, became popular.

That month, **Woman's Own** advised: *'First of all, do have it cut shortish. The shorter it is, the easier it is to manage, and it's fashionable, too, just now. You must have your hair thinned regularly, far too many of you let it grow wild, and it honestly doesn't pay ... Choose a style that you can manage yourself. The Dauphin bob is easy – big, loose curls which, if necessary, can be fitted over rollers, are all to the good. Shingled and swathed across the back is reasonable to deal with, and a "quiff" on the top in front.'*

Woman & Beauty, of November 1939, recommended short hair for women of all ages. For those in their twenties, it said: *'Don't choose too "fixy" a hairstyle – have one that won't collapse on you the day after it's set. Try a short, curly Astrakhan cut – or keep the back long, roll the side-pieces up, and put a crisp moiré bow on your topknot. Try tiny pearl earrings – you can buy them for 6d. a pair.'*

If you were in your 30s: *'Wear your hair short, and keep it tidy. And don't think that just because you aren't a girl-child any longer you can't wear a hair-ribbon. Try a little velvet one – you'll look charming and, thank Heaven, feminine!'*

'Eternal Youth' – a euphemism for those aged 40 and over – was an age where the secret was to – *'Keep your hair short and perfectly groomed.'*

Over the next year, hair styles became longer, but hair was kept strictly under control, with the back drawn up during the day, and only worn long for parties or other social occasions. The main inspiration for this style was the film actress, Veronica Lake, famous for her 'peek-a-boo' style, so-called because her long hair fell rather impractically over one eye.

'Pompadour curls', introduced in late 1940, were one variation: for this the long hair was drawn back from the ears, then swept upwards and fixed into 'big formal curls high on the top of the head' with the hair from the back being tucked underneath the side curls, where it was held in place with hair clips.

One drawback of changing hair styles was pointed out in a letter to **Woman** magazine of June 1942: *'Last week I put on a perfectly sound civilian gas mask and went into a police gas-van. I came out weeping from the effects of tear gas – and the reason was my hair. The expert told me that I was only one of many women who have not adjusted their gas masks for many months. Meanwhile we have adopted hair styles which feature masses of curls on top of the head and in some cases, at the sides as well. One sees many thick rolls going right round the head. The result is that gas masks do not fit as close to the face as is really necessary, which might mean casualties.'*

Variations of this style – long hair worn short by pinning it up on top – were fashionable for the next couple of years. **Good Housekeeping** wrote: *'the shoulder-length "bob", the off-the-face and the up-on-the-head-piled-high styles (are) leading in popularity.'* Another popular style was the page-boy, one variation being with the hair rolled in curls and brushed sleekly under. However, in mid-1943, shortages – most notably of shampoo and hairgrips – and the dangers of factory work led to the creation of new, shorter styles: *'Hair stylists are keen on shorter hair this season, so that we are likely to see short, soft curls in the nape of the neck, grouping down from the top of the ears, hair still back from the face but soft, with ends turned towards face, and a variety of arrangements on the brow-top. When next you have your permanent wave, decide on the style you like before having the hair cut for the permanent.*

'I don't think there's any denying that the cleverest and the most attractive and adaptable of the styles is the three-inch haircut which, properly done, even a child could manage ... The general principle is to cut the hair all over the head, so that none of it is more than three inches long. For the lucky ones with naturally curly hair that's the end, because all they then have to do is wash their hair and let it arrange itself. But for most of us, the next step is to have the head permed – quite lightly, please – so that it can be set into any way we like.

'To me this is the loveliest part of this short cut. There is no end to the styles in which it can be worn. You may think this is an exaggeration and that if your hair is very short there's not much you can do with it. But you'd be wrong because, believe it or not, I've seen elegant pompadours, neat rolls, baby curls, windswept effects, and the prettiest "bangs" – all with the basic three-inch cut.' Marjorie Gordon, **Home Companion**, September 1943.

There was also a 'party' version – *'brushed sleekly up at the sides and back and let loose in a soft bang over the forehead. And it stays that way, too, so you won't have to be for ever peering sideways into every mirror you pass, just to make sure you look all right. And even if the odd hair did get out of place, thanks to its shortness it wouldn't look mussed or untidy in the way that longer hair can. You'll find that formal or loose it still looks utterly charming, and right for any and every occasion.*

'Because of its adaptability this style is attractive on any head. It doesn't matter whether you're young

▼ The elaborate quiff, as seen here from 1943, either as part of a 'Dauphin', 'Pompadour', or otherwise, remained very popular throughout the war.

or old, stout or thin, or have even a head of snowy white hair. I'm sure you'd like it. To begin with, you'll need to experiment a bit with your sets to make sure you'd got the one that was most becoming to your features, but I can promise there will be no difficulty about this. I have yet to see an unsuccessful cut.'

However, Marjorie Gordon went on to stress that the cut had to be done correctly, a recurring theme in many of the more honest instructions on how to do the latest style: *'If you go to a good hairdresser you need have no qualms at all. It is important that the operator should be someone who knows the technique of cutting thoroughly, because it is on the cutting that the whole beauty of this short cut relies, so don't be tempted to try it out yourself at home!'*

▲ A variation of the short cut from **Mother** magazine, 1944. 'A halo of curls, radiating from the centre-back of your head – no parting at all.'

'I'm all for a simple version of the three-inch cut. Once done, when you wash your hair, all you have to do is set it in flat curls – preferably with a good setting lotion – and you'll find that when it is short like this the curls tend to stay in much longer, especially if you take the trouble of pinning it up each night.' **Home Companion**, June 1943.

Even the perm was unnecessary – Marjorie Gordon: *'Those with straight hair should have a perm after the cut, but strictly speaking that isn't really necessary if you have patience and a few curlers and pins or grips. I managed to keep my new cut quite successfully without a perm for several months. I found it necessary to pin up the hair every night, and my method was to give it a thorough brushing first and then pin it up all round the neck- line and behind the ears with ordinary hairpins – two pins per curl. If I felt extra energetic I did the whole head, but on the whole I found it more or less sufficient to do the back and sides.'*

The 3-inch cut, practical yet stylish, remained in vogue throughout the rest of the war, becoming the 2½-half inch cut by the time of VE day.

▼ Another somewhat startling forelock.

'Here's a hair style with a difference! The centre parting is continued all the way down the back, and the hair is swept softly up at the sides and front. The twin little plaits, tucked neatly under the roll, give it that 'fresh out of the bandbox' look.' **Woman's Weekly**, December, 1944. (left).

'Today's beauty is trim and practical, yet very feminine – like this charming hairstyle. The deep slanting waves across the front finish in softly rolled curls, while the sides and back are swept up neatly.' **Woman's Weekly**, December, 1944 (right).

'A quaint edition of the Edwardian hairstyle! Back and sides are brushed up smoothly, sweeping into soft rolls on top. The front roll is divided into five pin curls and they are left to fall softly over the brow.' **Woman's Weekly** November 1944. (below).

By 1944, **Housewife** magazine was advising its readers to look in the mirror before deciding on their preferred style:

'A new hair-do will get you out of the rut, off your shelf and into the swim quicker than anything else I know. Be as daring as you like in the choice of a new style, but remember that to be becoming it must make the face appear oval. If your face is long the arrangement of your hair should make it appear shorter. If it is round you must choose a style which will give it height. The square chin must be balanced by hair built out to make the forehead seem wider, the mature face must be given a lift with upswept hair, which is kind to sagging contours.

shredded soap, made for using as shampoo had to be added to hot water, then the two boiled until they became a thick liquid.

'The long face – Study the swept-forward style of the girl in the photograph and see how cleverly her face is shortened by those loose forehead curls. The tailored bang – the front hair cut in a fringe, waved and curled under-is another way of making a long face appear oval. A low side parting and the hair brushed smoothly across the head with a dip over the eyebrow and built-up temple curls is a third solution of the problem. Remember that if the hair is allowed to curl on to the forehead, it must be scooped up from temples and ears.

'The oval face – Lucky you, if your face is oval, for you can look well in any type of hair-do. The only danger is that of over-elaboration. Don't spoil the lovely oval of your face with curls or fringe. Keep the hair-line clear. If you're clever you'll choose a style which other women cannot copy – the simple Madonna style with centre parting, loose rippling waves, the back hair softly curled or knotted low at the neck. Remember, though, that a simple style needs perfect grooming, so spend the time that other women spend in setting innumerable pin curls in brushing your hair till it shines like satin.

'The mature face – Avoid fussy curls, tight waves and hair that drips on to the shoulders. Down-drooping curls and hair over the cheeks give an ageing droop to the whole face. Hair which is arranged in a knot or bun is also apt to be ageing, and the shingle cut is equally unbecoming, for the short cut at the nape draws attention to the back of the neck, seldom a plus-point after thirty-five. Medium short hair such as is worn by the woman in the picture is by far the most flattering length.

'The round face – To make the round face appear oval, pile the curls high on top of the head. The Edwardian and pompadour styles are particularly flattering to this type of face, but if you prefer a simple waved style, avoid horizontal waves. Bias waves give height.

'The square face – Like the round face, the hair should be drawn away from the cheeks and all fullness should be above the centre of the ears. To give balance to a face that is as wide at the chin as it is at the forehead, build up the hair where the head narrows. An asymmetrical effect – a roll of hair or curls built higher on one side than on the other is flattering to this type of face.' **Housewife**, April 1944.

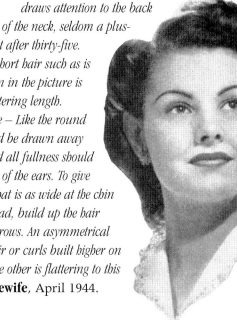

The next big innovation was the 'flat-top': *'Try yourself in one of these new flat-on-top hairstyles. They are new, youthful, easy to do, and such a change from the bunch of curls above the forehead that we've all been wearing.*

'When you try your new flat top style, keep the parting and the arrangement of the back hair as you wear them now; just begin the change by taking down any topknot of curls and smoothing your hair sleek and straight from the parting. Then, when you're used to yourself with your hair brushed flat, you can make a complete change in your hairstyle.

'Sleek and flat. A middle parting and the hair on each side of it brushed back off the face. The top and side hair converging into a roll or coil at the nape of the neck. This style is especially right for women with longer hair.' **Woman's Weekly**, December 1944.

'The centre-parted flat-top is a good style for any one with an oval or square face and regular features.

'Brush the hair very sleek and smooth each side of the centre parting and take it in with the side hair. Twist this side hair into a rope and lift it to the centre back where it must be pinned. If your hair is thick you can plait these side pieces instead of twining them, or simply plait together the ends of the centre back.

'If your forehead is narrow or your face seems rather short without its topknot, add two gay little bows, one each side.' **Mother**, May 1944.

'This is the new flat way of doing an upswept roll. From a side parting brush your hair flat and aslant across the top of your head, and twist the front hair in with the side pieces to form a roll. Make one long smooth roll all round your head, and if you feel the flat look takes getting used to, bring the roll high at the sides.

'A little bow or posy tucked in high at one side will give an impression of height without destroying the nice new flat look.

'This is a style for either a long face or a broad face and irregular features.' **Woman's Weekly**.

'I do envy women, especially the older ones, who have the courage to adopt a new fashion as soon as it comes out. I have dithered for months about changing

my hair-style to an Edwardian one and I took the plunge last week. Now I find all the newest hair-do's are flat across the top. Do you think they will catch on?

'With the young things, yes, but I cannot see the older women en-masse forsaking the Edwardian style. The upswept lines are so becoming to them.

'The flat-across the top style, in its present form, at any rate, is a trifle hard, and definitely ageing.' letter to **Woman & Home**, January 1945.

'Here's a version of the flat on top style that will suit any one with small features and a thin or long face. Divide off the front lock of hair and smooth it straight back from your forehead without a parting, like Alice in Wonderland. Pin the lock of your hair firmly to your head at the back to keep it flat, and brush out all the rest of your hair in feathery curls, bringing them high each side.

'Tie one of Alice's hair ribbons round your head to keep your hair tidily in place and then remove the grip at the back.' **Woman's Weekly**.

'Hair taken up into wings at the sides. Centre piece set into two slanting waves and four pin curls falling over the brow in a V shape. The back hair is curled over in a neat roll.' **Woman's Weekly**, January 1945.

'Soft roll curl in front and side hair waved and taken back off the face into a neat, tight chignon at the nape of the neck.' **Woman's Weekly**, January 1945.

Elaborate hairstyles often required a creative approach to accessories. 'Want to look your especial best for a party? Why not braid your hair with coloured ribbon, just for fun? The effect is charming and "little girl" and looks especially nice if your ribbons match your frock or are in a gay contrast to it.

'Or, if you haven't enough hair to braid, tuck what you have in a snood and bunch that snood with a posy of flowers that will perch among your curls. A half-yard square of fish net makes your snood for you – cut it from the biggest circle you can, run hat elastic or ribbon round the edges and there you are.

'But perhaps you don't wear a snood and instead brush your hair at the back into a soft V-shaped roll – if you do, tuck flowers into the "dip" and see how nicely they back you up for a party, or a big velvet bow pinned to the back of the head can be fun too.

'On hot nights, sweep the hair from the sides of your face and fix it up with crisp white bows of cotton *piqué – these will make a black frock look cool.*

'A black lace scarf thrown over your hair looks dreamy and romantic – this was called a Fascinator by Grandmamma (and perhaps she knew why).' **Home Companion,** July 1943.

▲ Typical girls' hair-styles, showing the two extremes – the straight bob, and the head full of curls and ringlets.

(above right) A teenage girl. The bubbly look was considered very fetching in girls of this age.

The advice for teenagers was a far cry from the gelled and sprayed options they prefer today: *'Avoid fussy, elaborate hairstyles, and see to it that your hair is always well brushed, beautifully clean and shining. Tie it up with a broad ribbon – polka dot, plaid, or what you please but make it fun.'* **Woman & Beauty,** November 1939.

Or: *'part your hair on one side, brush it back quite plainly, and catch the sides up with combs. This is a lovely style for anyone your age.'* **Home Companion,** May 1943.

Hair products changed and as with all else, many became difficult or impossible to get hold of. *'Hair brighteners have gone by the board. But have you tried the vegetable rinses which anyone can manage at home, and which will deal*

with those white hairs for you, or keep that parting reasonable? A vegetable dye is harmless. It washes off every time you shampoo and you won't get dry, brittle, and thin hair after using it. A vegetable rinse is cheap and anyone can afford it.' **Woman's Own,** December 1939. *'What a delight to see your hair gleaming with the new fashionable sheen, neat, smooth as silk. What a relief to know you can always get rid of the dull, dry, after-effects of a perm with Amami brilliantine. And if you are worrying about fading hair remember that Amami brilliantine restores natural colour. Four tones: Henna, Special Henna, Camomile, & Blue (for white hair).'* **Woman's Weekly**, December 1939. Reckitts blue, a clothes' dye, was one of the alternatives to proprietary products, in this case used by women with grey hair.

A healthy diet was also essential to beautiful hair; Evelyn Forbes, writing in **Housewife** magazine in August 1943, recommended *'... a cure for dull, lack-lustre hair. Soak three heaped dessertspoonfuls of oatmeal in twelve* *ounces of cold water overnight. In the morning, pour off the milky liquid and drink it. This contains silicon which the hair needs, and if the oatmeal water is taken every day, the hair will soon become delightfully glossy.'*

Hair curlers were used by all ages, as were hair nets. Many women routinely slept in curlers and hair nets. Women working in factories, catering or other environments where hair had to be kept off the face could wear their curlers during the day, covering the hair completely with a turban or scarf.

'Hair's a bit of a problem at nights, isn't it? Shampoos and sets are too precious to be wasted, so you must do something about keeping your crowning glory in order overnight. Curlers are fine if you can sleep in them, and the same goes for pins and grips (if you're lucky enough to have sufficient to pin up the whole of your head). Failing that, brush and comb your hair into place, slip on a hair net and over that tie a bandeau or scarf of fine cotton net, or, even better, of chiffon. You'll find that either of these grips on the net and stays put all night, no matter

how you toss about.' **Home Companion**, August 1943.

'An almost shoulder-length bob, just curled at the ends. Essential for this style: a young-looking face, a fairly long neck, thick hair kept scrupulously clean and brushed till it shines like silk. A permanent wave should not be necessary, as curling the ends is easy – your hairdresser will show you how. Vary it as follows:

'Centre parting, if you have good regular features. Bows fixed to Kirbigrips hold the hair back at the temples.

'Wear a wide bandeau and curl the ends under, page-boy fashion.' **Mother**,1944.

MEN'S HAIR

'I refer to Utility safety razor blades. Having used one with devastating effects, I can vouch for their general efficacy. I suggest that Mr Dalton should forthwith have all his surplus stock dropped on the enemy.' From a letter to Picture Post.

Men's haircuts were almost universally based on the traditional 'short back and sides', itself based on Army regulations; what showed outside the cap was the Army's business – 'get your 'air cut' – what was under it was yours. Therefore very short

at the back and sides and much longer on the top; and very different to the American crew-cut.

The long top could be parted in different ways: left, right and centre, though the most common was a side parting with the hair swept all the way across. To keep it there you needed hair dressing: brilliantine or one of a series of popular brands, such as Anzora, Nufix or Brylcreem, which became linked with the RAF, who, because of their reputation for looking sharp, were commonly called 'the Brylcreem Boys'. Some form of dressing was normal, even if your hair was one mass of tight curls, when you still had the standard cut but without the parting, the hair piling up on top.

Since Victorian times moustaches had been a sign that the wearer had served, or was serving, in the Army. Many ex-soldiers – of whom there

were millions from the First World War alone – still sported 'Old Bill'-type full moustaches. While these were only seen on men of advancing age, some middle-aged men wore full, but heavily-trimmed moustaches, and younger men tended to go bare-faced, or with the slight moustache known as a 'Ronald Coleman' after the dashing British-born Hollywood film star.

Sideburns hardly existed. Having a beard was a sign that you were either very old, a sailor, an eccentric, or an academic; the BBC's Drama Department had been evacuated to Evesham on the outbreak of war, where they were summed up as 'men in beards riding bicycles'. Beards tended to be full but trimmed; untrimmed beards being the sole province of bohemian artists or tramps. In 1939, debate raged over whether a beard obstructed the wearing of a gas mask and should therefore be shaved off. By 1940, when the threat of invasion dominated everyone's thoughts, and people looked suspiciously for disguised German paratroopers, anyone wearing a beard became the subject of intense suspicion from little boys and the Home Guard.

One strange decision in the maze of regulations which was rationing was that, unlike household soap or bath soap, shaving soap remained unrationed and, as such, joined the list of 'alternatives' to rationed or hard to get items.

A group of boys showing the short-back-and-sides at various stages of growth. The second boy from the left clearly shows the line between the long top and the rest.

◀ (bottom left) A popular style for those with tightly-curled hair.

▶ Men's hair tended to be heavily dressed with brilliantine or other preparations, such as Brylcreem

BRYLCREEM
The stuff to give the roots

IN HANDY JARS BOTTLES & TUBES **1'2½** *Larger bottles 1 9½, 2/1½ and 2 11½ All prices inclusive Purchase Tax.*

From retailers everywhere also N.A.A.F.I. and Service Canteens.

NO GUM · NO SOAP · NO SPIRIT · NO STARCH

County Perfumery Co., Ltd., North Circular Road, West Twyford, London, N.W.10

RAZOR BLADES

Razor blades were yet another victim of shortages. By 1942 men were limited to buying five razor blades each; on the black market they were selling for 42/- a gross, three-and-a-half times the legal maximum price.

In 1943, the government brought out Utility razor blades. One correspondent to Picture Post commented: *'Permit me, t*

hrough your columns, to congratulate the President of the Board of Trade upon discovering the perfect secret weapon. I refer, of course, to his Utility safety razor blades. Having used one with devastating effects, I can vouch for their general efficacy. I suggest that Mr Dalton should forthwith have all his surplus stock dropped on the enemy. I feel sure it would hasten the ending.'

Men would try to resharpen razor blades using the old trick of a glass tumbler. To do this you would dip the blade in warm water and hold it inside a glass lengthways with your finger along the centre of the blade. Then you would slowly revolve it around the inside of the glass for a dozen turns or so; it was said that by doing this you could make the blade last for almost a year.

In May 1944, **Hobbies Weekly** showed how to make a razor-blade sharpener from an old gramophone record: 'After using the sharpener the blade could be toned up by rubbing it in a glass.'

Record Blade Sharpener

SHARPENERS for safety razor blades can be made from old gramophone records—at least, you will be able to make one sharpener from each record, such as 10in. discs. The shape of the sharpener is shown, this being cut out with a metal-cutting fretsaw blade, although the usual fine fretsaw blade could be tried.

You need the plain "heart" of the record, for this surface is used for "stropping" the blades. If blunted slightly, i.e., if a blade has been used for shaving several times, it is first rubbed gently, in a circular motion, on the "track" end of the sharpener, this action removing most of the "burr" on the blade cutting edges, following which the blade is rubbed

on the plain surface, this giving the finishing touch to the blade.

However, before you can do so, the sharpener must be bent concave in the centre. To do so effectively, place the portion of record in a bath of warm water and, when the material becomes plastic, bend it to shape with the fingers.

It is a good idea to bend the material over the side of a large mug. There must be a slight curvature—not a deep one for the edges of the blades would thus be likely to "cut" up the surface of the record, particularly the tracking lines or sound grooves.

Now, it should be stated that the centre of most records are indented slightly where the label is adhered. This is not wanted. Choose a record that has no indentation, such as a Columbia record. You will likely find that the label is easily peeled off after having been immersed in the hot water.

In Use

Do not bother about the opposite side of the piece of record as this is not used. The concave curvature enables the cutting edges of the razor blades only to be touched. A slight pressure, with the fore-finger, is all that is necessary.

Naturally, the record material is not as good as a bakelite material, but the record provides you with grooved "honing" lines. The idea of this sharpener is based on the old dodge of using the inside of a drinking tumbler or glass. In fact, after rubbing the blade on the sharpener, it could be "toned up" by rubbing it in the glass.

When using the record sharpener, it could be dipped in cold water to lubricate the movement of the blade.

New Powder Shades from PARIS—

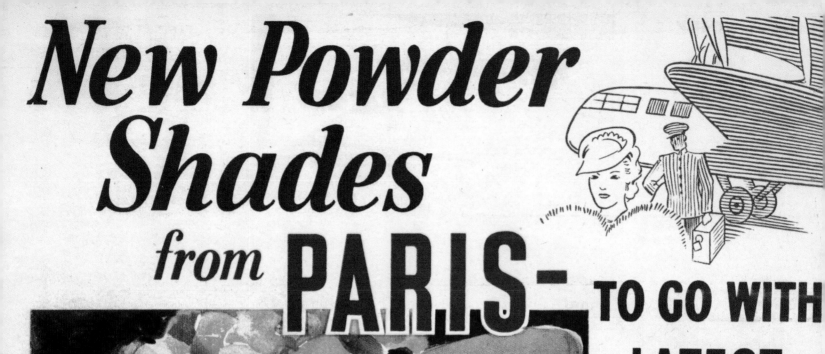

GLAMOROUS!

EXCITING!

...ING!

ROSE PEACH
Poudre
...KALON

TO GO WITH LATEST FASHIONS

THE Paris fashion shows reveal that this season's clothes demand entirely new complexion tones. Blended by a French Beauty Expert — with the help of a famous Paris Dress House — these very latest powder shades have been rushed to England. You can obtain them here only in the new thrilling shades of new Poudre Tokalon. "*Rose Peach*" is a subtly different rosy glow, lovely for blondes and mid-brunettes with fair complexions. "*Rachel*" — a true skin-tone shade for medium skins — neither very fair nor very dark. "*Brunette*" — richer, warmer shade, will make any dark-haired girl look seductive.

Poudre Tokalon is "air-floated" — which makes it ten times finer. Almost invisible on the skin — it looks *natural*. No "made-up" look. Perfumed with the fragrance of real flowers. And it stays on twice as long because blended with "Mousse of Cream" — a patented ingredient.

Try these new shades to-day. They are glamorous! exciting! daring! Each one gives your skin a life and radiance such as you have never achieved before. Remember, only in POUDRE TOKALON can you get these new Paris shades. The thrilling, flattering shades which give you the final touch of beauty every truly "chic" woman will have this season.

FREE By special arrangement any woman reader of this paper may obtain a de luxe Beauty Outfit

MAKE-UP

Initially, people assumed that make-up, like fashion, was too frivolous a matter for serious consideration in wartime. **Home Notes** of December 1939 wrote: *'Artificial make-up is, for the moment, at any rate, quite definitely "out". The movement for natural colouring started before the War, but there is no doubt that existing conditions have helped to encourage the fashion to look naturally glamorous rather than artificially.'*

It was not long before the cosmetics industry hit back. By February 1940, Tokalon Powder was advertising new colours: *'The Paris fashion shows reveal that this season's clothes demand entirely new complexion tones ... these very latest powder shades have been rushed to England ... "Rose Peach" is a subtly different rosy glow, lovely for blondes and mid-brunettes with fair complexions. "Rachel" a true skin-tone shade for medium skins – neither very fair nor very dark. "Brunette" – a richer, warmer shade, will make any dark-haired girl look seductive.'*

In the same edition of **Woman**, Pompeian face powder was advertised 'in six shades: Honey Rose, Rachel, Natural, Sun Rose, Brunette and Peach', while Tattoo lipstick was in nine shades: fire red, rose dawn, orchid, black magic, coral, exotic, natural, pastel and Hawaiian.

The following is the full treatment as recommended by various magazines and articles from the time.

'A stimulating luxurious bath to begin with, starting hot and cooling down just before you get out. Mix in some bath salts, or sea salts from the chemist, or ordinary mustard to give a tingle to your skin. Get out, and give yourself a sponge down as cold as you can take it, and a brisk rub all over with a rough towel.

'You've had cream on your face all this while. Now you can wipe it away and splash your face with ice-cold water or astringent. Put a little heap of special toilet oatmeal in the palm of each hand and rub it over your face or give yourself a face pack,

or massage your cheeks before you remove the cream with a soft scrubbing brush.' **Woman**, October 1941.

'If you're feeling harassed and your brow won't smooth, use a little cream and a rubber forehead strap. Ten minutes, and you'll emerge with a cloudless brow. The joy is you can use it when you're dressed without getting untidy.' **Woman & Beauty**, November 1939.

Much of the advice shows skin was treated rather more roughly than would be acceptable today: *'Make a lather of your very finest, blandest soap, and with a very, very soft nail brush, rubber brush, soap mat or soft loofah, rub the lather gently into your face, using upward circular movements along all the lines – nose to mouth lines, frown lines and up across cheeks.*

'Now is the time, if you have saved a precious face pack, to use it with best effect. Perhaps you have a teaspoon or two of fuller's earth which you can mix with water and put on your face. If you haven't a face pack, press out the blackheads after holding your face in the steam of hot water, then do some vigorous massage.

'Slap your cheeks with alternate hands, giving a gentle upwards push at the end of each slap. Put the bottom of each palm under each eyebrow bone and push upwards to lift the flesh which forms furrows between the eyes. Tap the skin under your eyes with butterfly lightness. After five minutes the skin should feel tacky.

'Then take a wet flannel wrung out in cold water and slap your cheeks with that. Pat your face dry after the cold slapping and apply your foundation. A fine milk is soothing and non-greasy and suitable for most skins, but sometimes a very dry skin can take a cream foundation. Vanishing cream should only be used round the sides of your nose and on the chin, where shine comes first.' **Mother**, May 1944.

An alternative DIY face pack: *'excellent for toning up a tired skin and for removing discolouration'*, could be made by beating the white of a fresh egg to a stiff froth, then adding half a teaspoonful of fresh lemon juice. The results should be applied to the skin of face and neck and left for 20 minutes.

The eyes, too, could be enhanced with home-made lotions: *'if your favourite eye lotion is unobtainable you can work wonders with boracic lotion. Put a dessertspoonful of boracic crystals in a jug, pour on a pint of boiling water; then, when the water has cooled, strain it off and bottle it for daily use, just as it is, in your eye bath.'* Or, alternatively a solution of salt in water: *'Then, even the loveliest eyes are enhanced by careful grooming of brows and lashes. A touch of oil can do unbelievable things to your eyelashes. It will not only make them soft and lustrous immediately, it will help them to grow. So put a spot of salad oil or olive oil or (best of all) castor oil in an egg cup and give those eyebrows and lashes a nightly grooming with a little paint brush.'* **Home Notes**, September 1942.

Teeth could be whitened with home-made preparations: *'First of all, a sage wash to make those teeth even more sparklingly white. All you have to do is to pour hot water on to a few dried sage leaves and leave until it is cold. Strain off – and you have a lotion which, massaged into teeth and gums, will make your teeth really like pearls.'* **Home Notes**. And in the absence of toothpaste, many used soot to do the job!

Make-up depended on the weather: *'In a heat wave wear a light make-up, and do your face more often than usual during the day. It's a good plan to lighten your beauty preparations, adding a little rose or distilled water to foundation lotion and complexion milk, and a few drops of Eau de Cologne to your creams.'* **Home Companion**, August 1943.

It also depended on the seasons. Marjorie Gordon, writing in that November's issue: *'Of course, you don't use the same technique with your make-up in winter as you do in summer. It's obvious that not only for looks but for protection the skin needs something different – something more. I have found (and my skin is a fairly normal, average one) that in very cold weather a thin cream isn't sufficient protection and that it not only doesn't hold my powder properly but also it doesn't keep my complexion from getting rough. So when the hard frosts start I switch to a heavier cream and the one I use is a skin-food – the kind you apply at nights – only for foundation purposes I use much less. 'The merest layer is enough and I always make sure that there's no stickiness left by wiping gently over the face with a piece of soft linen. What cream remains holds the powder quite effectively.'*

There were two types of rouge, equivalent today to blusher: cream rouge, put on under the face powder, and powder rouge, worn over the powder. You could, of course, use both: *'Your rouge will last better if you use a spot of cream rouge and work it well into your foundation cream. Then apply powder and last of all add a little powder rouge. When powder rouge wears off, the cream one will take its place.'* **Woman's Weekly**, December 1944.

'Put your powder rouge on with a tiny velvet puff, then smooth it carefully with your fingertips. See that the colour fades naturally, and leaves no harsh edges. Don't make the mistake of dabbing on too much rouge, will you? The warmth of your skin will deepen the colour for you, you'll find, so be sparing.' **The Lady's Companion**. Once you have done this: *'dust on a light film of powder. This will make your "colour" look as if it came from within, just as Nature's does.'*

Seasonal variations dictated that: *'In summer pinky shades of rouge and lipstick are cooler looking than vermilion shades.'* While: *'In winter you need less rouge than in summer. Reason? Well, the cold usually whips some colour into the palest skin, and if you're over generous with the artificial colouring you run the risk of looking rather hectic.'* **Home Companion.**

Difficulties in getting cosmetics were compounded by the need for them to match: *'Never make the mistake of using a rouge and lipstick that weren't specially designed to go one with t'other by the makers – it's as bad as mixing bright scarlet geraniums with a bowlful of dusky red roses!'* **The Lady's Companion**.

But *'If you're absolutely stuck for matching rouge, why not use your lipstick? It's not quite the same consistency as a cream rouge, but it does do the job, and it looks better than going pale, or, much worse, using a clashing rouge. Providing you use a slightly greasy foundation cream, it works.'* **Home Companion**, January 1943.

A variation was to add a few drops of warm almond oil to melted down lipstick ends. Now, powder: *'Put it on with a clean tuft of cotton wool, and start powdering at your neck, finishing last with your forehead. Don't powder your eyelids.'* **The Lady's Companion**. Alternatively: *'Puff on your powder, beginning with forehead, then chin and last of all your nose. Use a lighter shade of powder for your fairer skin.'* **Mother**, May 1944.

In the summer: *'remember to darken your powder as your skin develops its tan ... You can keep adding a little of the suntan powder to your usual shade until you can use it neat.'* **Mother and Home**, June 1941. Suntan powder was a suntan shade of face powder, such as 'Dark Brunette'.

By autumn – *'You'll probably notice that the time has come to put away old suntan powder and revert to a paler one for the winter. You know, of course, that if you can't get powder the exact shade of your skin, it is wise to choose one slightly darker – never lighter ... If you don't, and you get cold, your skin will take on an ashen look and make you appear ghostly. Avoid anything with a yellowish tinge or you'll look green. Yes, I know that in summer you probably do look a wow with that banana shade, but it is definitely only for sunny weather.'* Marjorie Gordon.

Advice on choosing lipstick was much the same as now: *'Try it on the back of your hand, and before you buy it, make very sure it matches up to the colour pigment in your skin.'* It went on: *'Make sure your lipstick has an olive oil foundation – besides acting as a kindly protection against drying February winds, the olive oil will give your mouth a soft gleaming appearance which is very attractive. 'Pencil in the colour lightly, then to see it's evenly put on, smooth it in carefully with your little finger. If your mouth is on the thin, straight side, give it a prettier curve by emphasising a cupid's bow. Thick lips need only the lightest film of colour, and this should not be taken to the extreme edges. Never put any colour in the corners of a mouth which has a downward curve.'* **The Lady's Companion**, February 1940.

'... do you know that you can "blot" your lips to flower-petal smoothness after applying the colour,

and so make it last all day? Just the tiniest scrap of soft paper will do, or even the corner of an old handkerchief. Place it between your lips, press them firmly together for a moment or two.' **Home Notes,**

September 1942. Or: *'Paint in the delicate curves with a camel-hair brush, smooth the colour well in with your fingertip, then blot your mouth on a tissue and if you want a bloom like a peach, just dust your lips with powder.'* **Woman**, December 1940.

Once again there were seasonal changes: *'Careful with that lipstick in winter. No orange shades, please, and no cyclamen [an orangey-pink] unless you're quite positive it doesn't make your skin look blue. It's much safer to stick to clear reds and pinks, and, it's wise to be a little more sparing than usual. But don't think that leaving lipstick off altogether will make you look warmer. The reverse would, in fact, be true, because colourless lips nearly always look cold and cheerless, and are inclined to give the face a pinched appearance, which is the very thing you're trying to, avoid.'* **Home Companion**, November 1943. While in summer: *'pinky-red and cyclamen tints look all wrong with an outdoor complexion. Vivid scarlet is often the young girl's choice with a tanned skin, but a soft, brownish red is twice as becoming.'* **Mother and Home**, June 1941.

As the war progressed, all make-up became very expensive and hard to get, especially lipstick, as this reader's letter published in **Home Companion**, in March 1943, demonstrates: *'Where I live in the country it's very difficult to get cosmetics of any kind, and lipsticks are scarcest of all. I've got several lipstick ends, how can I use them up?'* – *'Scoop all the ends out of their holders and put them on a saucer or some sort of container over a saucepan of boiling water. Let them melt down until, with the end of a nail file or something like that, you can easily mix them into a stiff paste. Then put this back into a lipstick holder, packing the paste well down. Give the lipstick a day or two to firm up, and you'll find that it works perfectly well.'*

With the disappearance of make-up from the shops, a clear complexion became all the more necessary.

Woman's Weekly, in December 1944, showed how to get the most out of your lipstick with a forerunner of today's lip brushes: *'Isn't it just too heartbreaking when your favourite, irreplaceable lipstick is reduced to the very end? Did you know that you can use the very end in the container if you paint it on with a camel hair brush? Get*

A CHART FROM *THE LADY'S COMPANION*, GIVING THE CORRECT MAKE-UP FOR DIFFERENT COLOURING

Redheads
Lipstick, Orange
Rouge, Orange

Blondes
Lipstick, Naturelle
Rouge, Cherry

Light Brunettes
Lipstick, Miami
Rouge, Scarlet

Medium Brunettes
Lipstick, Boulevard
Rouge, Brunette

Dark Brunettes
Lipstick, Lido
Rouge, Medium

Black Hair
Lipstick, Everglades
Rouge, Raspberry

a firm brush and rub it on the stump, and then draw the line of your mouth with care before filling it in. Apart from salvage value, you'll be surprised at the thin clarity of the make-up. It looks so natural.'

The 'Gardenia Look' called for cherry coloured cream rouge, cameo powder, cherry lipstick, green eyeshadow and mascara. However, by the middle years of the war beggars could not be choosers – you took whatever was in the shops, as the following extract from Mass Observation shows:

'Cosmetics are much discussed. There is always great excitement when the news goes round that some particularly popular brand of any kind of cosmetic is in stock somewhere.'

"They've got some Coty powder in J's."
"What do you mean, real Coty? In the Coty boxes?"
"I think so. I haven't been but Lil went dinner time, and she got a lovely box."
"What shades have they got?"
"I don't know ..."
"Are there any dark shades? I want a dark powder for the summer."
"I shan't worry about the colour. So long as it's Coty, that's all I care. I'll mix it to make the right colour."
"Will it still be there tomorrow? Was there a lot?"
"I don't know, Lil said ..."
"I'm not going to chance it. I'm going to get off early tonight."
"It's worth it for Coty isn't it? You don't see that much now."

Next, the eyes: *'Pluck your eyebrows to a groomed line, and brush them lightly with oil to make them glisten. Remember that the way you shape them can alter the whole appearance of your face.'* **Woman**, December 1940.

'For eyebrow plucking you will need eyebrow tweezers, hand-mirror, boiling water, a wool-wrapped orange-stick, peroxide of hydrogen, a stick of menthol and eyebrow or mascara brush. Sterilise your tweezers in the boiling water, and rub the menthol stick over your eyebrows, to deaden the pain and make the straggling hairs easier to see. Brush the eyebrows downwards and remove any straggling hairs which spoil the line of the eyebrow. Be careful not to flatten the eyebrows on to the nose, but remove any hairs which grow across the bridge of the nose.

'Tweezers in one hand and hand-mirror in the other, grasp the offending hair firmly and give it a sharp tug in the direction in which it grows. As each hair is removed, touch the place with the wool-wrapped orange-stick dipped in peroxide. Now brush the brows upwards and pluck beneath them in the same way. Wipe off the menthol and brush the eyebrows into shape. If they are inclined to be pale or scanty, paint them with castor oil each night for a month.' **Good Housekeeping**, February 1944.

Now you were ready for make-up: *'Perhaps you fight shy of mascara? You vaguely think it's "fast" – but any woman who understands the value of make-up knows it enhances her appearance tremendously.'* **The Lady's Companion**, February 1940. Mascara was only to be applied to the upper lashes. If you could not get mascara, there were substitutes – a soft blacklead pencil, or even moustache wax, boot-polish or burnt cork, then: *'When the mascara has dried, take up a spot of brilliantine or Vaseline on your brush and trace it lightly over the brows to soften the effect.'* **Woman and Home**, January 1945.

'For parties ... smear a little brilliantine or cold cream on your lids to make the eyes look larger.' **Home Companion**, September, 1943. An alter-

native was Vaseline. This worked well, but if it got hot the Vaseline became sticky, making it very difficult to close your eyes and impossible to blink! Then: *'If you're skilful you can apply a little eye shadow to your lids, but please only do it very sparingly and then only if you're going to be in artificial light. Otherwise you run the risk of looking heavy-eyed and sleepy!'*

In December 1939, **Home Notes** magazine reported: *'It is because so many people are having to use their hands for practical work of various kinds, that a vogue has started for well-manicured but sensible finger-tips. Everywhere one sees smart women with quite short – if perfectly shaped – fingernails and the softer shades of nail varnish are definitely in demand.'*

Long nails became a sign that their wearer was certainly not 'doing their bit', as such they were to be avoided. Popular nail varnish colours early in the war were soft, smoky tones, such as, Cameo, Regency, French Rose and Laurel. By 1943, nail varnish had all disappeared, however: *'You can polish your nails with one of the powder nail polishes, though. They impart a lovely waterproof gloss and tint the nails a delicate rose pink.'* To put this on: *'See that your hands and nails are perfectly dry before using powder polish. All you have to do is sprinkle a little of the powder into the palm of the hand and then brush the nails lightly over it with a backward and forward movement.'* **Woman's Weekly.**

Then they needed to be polished up to a high shine, but: *'A buffer ... is out of the question – but a wee square of wash-leather or a tiny "cushion" of wash leather, stuffed with cotton-wool, is an excellent substitute.'* **Home Chat**, December 1943.

Alternatively you could make one out of an old toothbrush by padding the head with cotton wool and then covering it with a small piece of chamois leather. Or simpler still, you could make a fingerstall from an old chamois glove and polish the nails with this.

You can still have finger-tip beauty

Sorry, no more Cutex liquid nail polish —not until after the war. But there's Cutex powder polish to bring lasting lustre to the natural beauty of your finger nails.

MADE BY THE CREATORS OF CUTEX LIQUID NAIL POLISH

▲ Liquid nail varnish was banned in the latter part of the war, being replaced by powder varnish, as advertised here.

By 1944 liquid nail varnish was no longer available at all. *'Manicurists are not allowed to use varnish these days'* reported **Woman's Weekly,** and by 1945, you often had to make do with nothing at all except a good brushing. Once again an old toothbrush did the trick, using a little soap and a circular movement to brush the entire surface of each nail several times a day. This was supplemented by rubbing the nails briskly across the palm of the opposite hand at odd moments to enhance their natural shine.

In December 1939, **Woman's Own** recommended hairstyles and make-up for women in the Services.

'1 The uniform of the A.T.S. is khaki, and to go with it you should choose a liquid powder foundation and powder over it with a warmish peach powder. Lipstick is allowed, but please buy a natural one, with rouge to match. Have your hair arranged in flattish curls in front and shingled at the back

'2 The handkerchief cap of the V.A.D. suits almost any style of hair, but hanging curls are probably the easiest to manage. Wear English rose make-up, natural powder, and English rose lipstick and rouge. This make-up suits the quiet trimness of the nursing uniform better than anything.

'3 Are you a member of the W.R.N.S.? Then brush the hair up from the face – it goes best with the hat – and have a roll at the back. Choose a liquid make-up: It lasts splendidly and is ideal for the woman on duty who hasn't much time to "tittivate". Powder to tone, and use a very natural rouge and lipstick.

'4 If you're an A.R.P. warden, have your hair cut fairly closely, and if you can indulge in a perm of "bubbles", do, because this is the ideal dressing for the tin hat! Choose a cream of roses foundation, a warm brown powder, and just a touch of Auxiliary red lipstick and rouge.'

If you worked in an office: *'He'll hate to see you making-up or fussing over your face in work hours, but he'll notice the moment your face shines. Use an astringent liberally first thing in the morning (witch-hazel will do), splashing it all over your face. Then a milk or special foundation, not cream*

because it gets greasy when you're hot, a liquid rouge because it can't smear and finally your powder.' **Woman**, October 1941.

Then as now, the first problem for teenagers was spots. As now, diet was often the solution: *'Persistent spots mean disordered blood, and often the cure lies in a simple diet. In your menus avoid all fried foods, fish, breads, potatoes, buns, pastry, floury puddings, sweets, and chocolate.*

'Concentrate instead on plenty of fresh green vegetables, salads, fresh and stewed fruit. Eat meat sparingly, and avoid soups other than the clear or vegetable broth variety. Drink weak tea or milk, or freshly pressed fruit juices. Follow these suggestions for three weeks, and I promise you you'll see an enormous difference in the condition of your skin. Avoid constipation at all costs, won't you – all spot-sufferers would do well to cultivate the "morning salts" habit twice a week, and another important "must" is drink at least six tumblers of cold water each day.' **Home Companion.**

Then there was keeping the skin clean: *'Wash the skin always with sulphur soap – all chemists keep it, and it's not a bit expensive. After washing, bathe the face in cold water, pat dry very gently, then dab with eau de Cologne. Please, please try and resist using make-up till your skin is clear. For special occasions you can always hide up the blemishes with calamine lotion or a "spot-stick". When you go to bed, cleanse with your sulphur soap again, and before retiring paint over your skin with a mixture of glycerine and ichthyol. Again your chemist will be able to sell it to you quite cheaply. If the pores are in very bad condition, a reliable pore paste or a simple mask will often work wonders, and both are still obtainable today.'* **Good Housekeeping.**

An almost universal problem was the subject of teenage girls and make-up: *'We may as well touch on the vexed problem of make-up. This is mainly vexed owing to the fact that many mothers can't help resenting their daughters using it because it is a sign that they are growing up. It is unwise, however, to forbid make-up or even to make much fuss about it, or, as I have said, you may find your girl piling it on! Instead, encourage her own natural good taste, advise her to use really good brands and point out that applying her powder and lipstick is an art.'*

▼ For many women, soap became the only daily make-up available, although even soap went 'on the ration'.

This article, from February 1943's **Good Housekeeping**, sees mothers as the main objectors, although in many cases it was father who complained that girls wearing make-up were, to coin a baffling phrase then in common use, 'no better than they should be'!

Being the traditional age for rebellion, many teenage girls took to experimentation with make-up, putting it on after they had left home, and being careful to rub it off before they returned. The result was rarely well done. **The Lady's Companion** wisely suggested: *'Now if our young Miss Seventeen is to make the best of this joyous springtime of her life and looks, she must remain her pretty natural self. Not for her are rouges to dim the first roses ... her bright young eyes must remain innocent of eye-shadow and mascara yet. A pretty pastel lipstick, a little cream and powder – that is all she must allow herself. Her hair must be dressed simply but becomingly – brushed and brushed till it sheens and ripples like a field of corn a'blow.'*

Almost from the start of the war, make-up came under attack from two different official quarters. The first was the Board of Trade, who, in order to save scarce raw materials and cut down on the amount of manpower used in producing 'luxuries' generated a storm of 'Orders', which limited the amounts of certain goods that could be produced. In June 1940 came the Limitation of Supplies (Miscellaneous) Order, under which manufacturers and wholesalers were forbidden to sell to retailers in the home market goods in excess of two-thirds of the value of those sold during the last six months of 1939. In December 1940 the order was revised and the sale of more essential goods was reduced to one half, while the sale of less essential goods was restricted to a quarter.

The second official attack on cosmetics came through the treasury. Heavy taxation was needed to finance the war, and purchase tax on non-necessities was a good way to raise revenues. On October 21, 1940, this was introduced for many goods, at rates varying from 16 to 33 per cent. Then on April 14, 1942, came the 'Sacrifices for Victory' budget: purchase tax on a number of luxury goods doubled, while in the budget of April, 1943, purchase tax went up once more to 100 per cent on luxury items; prices of cosmetics rose by 50 per cent.

As an example we can compare the rise in prices of a few common cosmetics over the course of the war (remember this a time when many prices were controlled to stop inflation). Tattoo lipstick sold at 4/6 early in 1940, going up to 5/6 by the end of 1941 and reaching 7/6 by the end of 1944. Pompeian cold cream and vanishing cream sold at 6d each in late 1939 rising to 7$\frac{1}{2}$d each in late 1941, 9d each in early 1943, and 10$\frac{1}{2}$d each by early 1945, while a small bottle of Miner's Liquid Make-up cost 7$\frac{1}{2}$d in 1941, 9d in September 1942, 10$\frac{1}{2}$d in June 1943, and 1/2 in January 1945. These increases average over 75 per cent.

All this of course created a thriving black market in cosmetics. Robberies became common. Often whole consignments would be hijacked in transit, to turn up being sold by spivs at inflated prices. With big profits to be made, home-made preparations, claiming to be well-known brands appeared, complete with fake labelling, apparently having 'fallen off the back of a lorry' (probably sold out of suitcases in Oxford Street – little changes!). Some of the products appearing on the street were made from extremely dangerous ingredients, and the Ministry of Information produced a short film, **Black Market Beauties,** graphically showing the harmful effects of these products.

On the other hand there was an increasing amount of 'tips' on making your own, safe, alternatives, produced by official bodies and in newspapers and magazines. **101 Ways to Save Money in Wartime**, a booklet issued by the National Savings Movement, included such advice as: *'When applying cold cream, do so with a piece of cotton wool dipped in cold water; it will go twice as far.'*

'Before using a new pack of cotton wool, unroll it

▼ With the disappearance of make-up from the shops, a clear complexion became all the more necessary.

and place it in front of the fire (not too near to be danger-ous). The heat will cause it to swell to twice the size and it will last longer.

'When the milk supply is back to normal, try this inex-pensive yet efficient beauty treatment. Mix a level teaspoon-ful of salt with two tablespoonsful of milk and rub it gently over the skin. Allow it to dry and leave it on all night.

'Carrot juice is excellent for the complexion and helps to correct any tendency to corpulence, while cucumber juice is one of the finest slimming cures.

'Deodorants are most important factors in saving; quite apart from the hygiene angle their regular use means longer life for coats, dresses, lingerie, etc. Many of the well-known brands are difficult to obtain at the moment, but Witchhazel or powdered bicarbonate of soda are reason-ably effective in most cases.'

Other common alternatives were beetroot juice applied to the lips and 'sealed' with vaseline as a substitute for lipstick, starch instead of face pow-der, and calamine lotion instead of foundation.

By August 1942 shortages were so severe that the Ministry of Supply went so far as to issue its female munitions workers an allowance of a high grade foundation and face powder along with a booklet, **R.O.F. Beauty Hints. Look to your Looks**. Industry provided good sources for replacements; when nail varnish became unprocureable, dope, varnish, or even paint could all be made to serve.

Home Chat magazine's Christmas number gave recommendations for Christmas presents: 'Boxes of powder, these days, are a very "safe" gift, for no longer are women ultra-particular that their powder has a certain perfume. The box will come in its wartime wrapping, and here's where you can do wonders to make it gay and sea-sonable – wrapping it in a wee square of gay paper, or teaming it up with a chiffon or lace "hankie" puff. They cost coupons to buy, so make the hankie from those scraps left from a dance frock, "rolling" the edge finely and stitch-ing a little wool puff in the centre. Wool puffs are nicer, far, than swansdown ones, which so often leave bits.

'A lovely duet – a really "super" gift for wartime is a box of peach powder and a jar of foundation cream. The two together give the skin such a delicate bloom. Cold cream, hand cream – both will be welcome gifts – doubly welcome to the girl whose war-time job is taking toll of her hands. And that reminds me, tuck in with the cream a pair of sleeping mitts – made from an odd scrap of soft silk.'

The **Home Companion** gave another tip to avoid replacing a powder puff: 'Powder puffs were made to be washed, whether they're swansdown or wool or cotton. a clean puff is more economical with your powder; it uses less, and in these days of expensive and scarce cosmetics, that's a big consideration.'

Good Housekeeping recommended the kitchen as an excellent source for cosmetic substitutes: 'A few minutes to spare and half a pound of prunes in the cupboard? Then make this Swedish complexion drink. Split and stone the prunes, put them in a saucepan with a quart of water, an ounce of sugar and the rind of an orange or lemon. Boil rapidly for two minutes, simmer for half an hour, strain, and, if possible, add the juice of an orange or lemon. serve cold.

'Sour milk may be a domestic tragedy, but it is also a beauty find. Strain off the lumpy curds and use the clear liquid which remains to wipe over your face, neck and hands. The lactic acid it contains will bleach the skin and whiten a sallow neck. Keep the face wet with the liquid for five minutes.

'The next time you have cucumber, save the end piece and rub the cut surface over face, neck and hands, allow-ing the juice to dry on the skin. Cucumber juice is whiten-ing and an astringent.

'Perhaps you're making a batch of rolls or tea cakes? Save some of the yeast for your looks. A couple of teaspoon-fuls dissolved in a cupful of milk makes a pore-cleansing, skin-refining face mask. If your skin is dry, try adding one part fine oatmeal to four parts of your face powder. A paste of oatmeal and milk used in place of soap will chase away any blackheads.'

The reality of the shortages was that often peo-ple were forced to do without any make-up. Like stockings, if you could get hold of make-up it was saved for special occasions. It was, of course, less of a bind because everyone else was in the same boat. Once again 'Artificial make-up is, for the moment, at any rate, quite definitely "out", but now, what had in 1939, been a fashion statement, was now merely a statement of fact.

'Real beauty the 1943 way is beauty that springs from radiant health – the kid that means sparkling clear eyes, a smooth, supple skin, glossy hair and a figure that gets its good lines not from strong elastic but from well condi-tioned muscles.

'With the shortage of cosmetics as great as it is, it is essential that we should try to get our skins into such a con-

dition that we aren't embarrassed by having to do with fewer beauty aids.' **Home Companion**, July 1943; and from another article from 1943: *'if you've been caring for [your skin] aright during the past it shouldn't look anything but fresh and attractive without make-up.'*

This fitted in with the Ministry of Food's push on health and fitness: *'An ounce of cabbage is worth an inch of lipstick.'* Thus the three strands of beauty became; good diet, exercise, and cleanliness: *'To put more make-up on a face that's probably not perfectly clean and shows signs of the day's work will never make you fresh. Much better go and have a thorough good wash and finish it with a rinse in cold water. If you can rinse your face in this way for about two minutes, splashing and patting the water into your skin (not forgetting your neck), you'll feel a whole lot refreshed and, what's more, your new make-up will go on better and stay smooth and mat for the rest of the evening.'* **Home Companion**, July 1943.

Domestic soap joined the ever expanding list of rationed goods on February 9, 1942, due to the shortage of fats used in its manufacture. Just like clothes rationing it was announced with no fore-warning. Everybody was allowed four coupons for each four-week period, which could be used for toilet soap, hard soap, soap powder or soap flakes. There was no need for registration, so coupons could be used in any shop. The yellow ration book supplement, R.B. 9, provided the coupons, which were to be cancelled by the shopkeeper rather than cut out.

You had a choice, either 4 ounces of household soap or 2 ounces of toilet soap per person per month. This of course included soap for washing-up, although surprisingly it did not include men's shaving soap, and many people washed their face with it.

The usual flood of good advice followed. The booklet, **101 Ways to Save Money in Wartime**,

issued by the National Savings Movement, included: *'A pint of boiling water poured over a handful of sage leaves, bottled and mixed with soap flakes as required, will give you an excellent tonic shampoo.*

'Of course hard water means more soap, so 'Inexpensive bath-water softener can be made by making up a strong solution of carbonate of soda or washing soda crystals and adding half ounce of verbena or oil of lavender.'

A **Lux** advert from November 1942 suggested: *'To make your Lux Toilet Soap last longer. Follow these simple hints. Always keep soap dry. When not in use, place your Lux Toilet Soap tablet on a little rubber mat, if you have one, or in a wire tray. This keeps it dry – saves waste.*

'Never let soap lie about in the bath or basin. It's wasteful to leave your soap in the water. So use what is necessary and then put the tablet back on its rubber mat or in its tray.

'Don't use a flannel. Instead of rubbing the soap on to a flannel, rub it on your hands. Then, with your soapy hands, you can wash your face and body.

'Save your left-overs. When you are nearing the end of a tablet of soap, stick what is left on to the new tablet. Pressed down firmly, it will not come unstuck and you will not waste even the tiniest bit of soap.'

All the same, **Instructions for American Servicemen in Britain** written in 1942, included: *'One of the things the English always had enough of in the past was soap. Now it is so scarce that girls working in the factories often cannot get the grease off their hands or out of their hair.'*

Not only soap was in short supply. Bath water itself became 'rationed' when, in 1942, in order to save the fuel used in heating water, the government introduced the '5 inches of water' scheme. The public were encouraged to limit their baths to no more than 5 inches of water, opening the door for many a ribald joke about the water not covering one's requirements. The government's advice was to have a daily rub-down while standing in a bowl of water, saving the bath for a weekly soak.

THE FIGURE

In the years immediately after the First World War, the preferred silhouette for female fashions was for a boyish figure. During the 'thirties, femininity came back in fashion and by the start of the Second World War, the preferred shape was more natural, although still slim, with square shoulders. Many relied on artificial help, such as corsets or padded shoulders, although women's magazines regularly advertised methods of achieving 'the perfect bust' in three weeks, or, for either sex, adding 3 inches to your height, in a similarly improbable time frame.

On the editorial pages, advice was far more realistic: *'Exercises, designed to strengthen the muscles in your breast will correct both a small or large bust. Don't attempt massage, it can be very dangerous unless it is done by an expert, and be careful of bust improving gadgets; the only safe method of bust reducing is by exercise.'* **Woman**, October 1940.

'Figure faults bother the young girl as acutely as the older woman. A heavy bust can make her miserable, and so can thick legs and ankles. The bust is made up largely of delicate glands, so for this reason nothing much can be done about altering the size, but with a good type of supporting brassiere, which encourages the muscles to do their work properly, much can be done to acquire graceful firmness. Teach her also to keep a watch on posture. There are corrective exercises for the bust as for other figure faults, including heavy legs and ankles which may also arise from bad posture habits.

'Keep your head high when you are up, low when you're in bed, and you'll never suffer from a double chin.

▶ Magazines were full of adverts promising ideal shapes in ridiculous time frames.

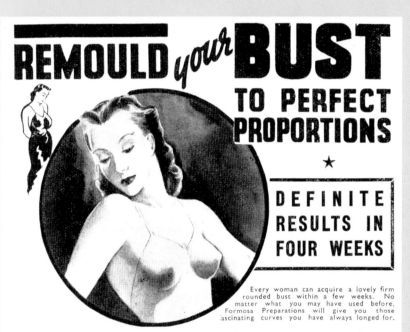

'Keep your chest up when standing, sitting or walking, and diaphragm bulge and thickened waist won't mean a thing to you. Throw your hips forward, and your spine will automatically straighten, your tummy will flatten and your tail will tuck under in its proper place.' **Good Housekeeping,** February 1943.

Letters on the problem pages of women's magazines show posture was a major concern: *'What can be done for sagging breasts after childbirth? Nothing should be done at all until after the weaning period, and even then exercises cannot be guaranteed to correct the sag. But do try this one, night and morning, for a few minutes each session. Take position standing or sitting, lift arms to shoulder height, bend elbows with hands touching shoulder front, pressing just above arm-pits. Now with a brisk movement, body well upright, fling the arm outward and upward. Tense muscles of the arm, then bring hand back to the original position. Repeat movement with right arm, and alternately.'* **Good Housekeeping,** February 1944.

'And here's an exercise for round shoulders. Stand erect with your arms by your sides. Now bend the elbows and place the tips of your fingers on your shoulders. Then circle the arms, using the shoulders as pivots, and trying to make the shoulder blades meet at the back. Do this exercise both backwards and forwards. To begin with you

▼ The ideal woman's shape of the forties. Note the square shoulders, and a bust much smaller than would be required for today's pin-ups.

may find it easier to move one arm at a time.'
Home Companion, August 1943. Other advice for the round-shouldered included sleeping without a pillow.

In his book, **Keep Fit in Wartime**, Dr Harry Roberts recommended gardening: *'Of all the recreative hobbies that a man or a woman can pursue, I can think of none so capable of yielding to its devotee anything like the measure of physi-*

cal health, mental stimulus, and emotional pleasure as gardening. There is now unlimited opportunity for combining healthy recreation with genuine, useful war work. The slogan "Grow More Food" is an exhortation to health as well as to helpfulness.

'Gardening is, moreover, a hobby not for the young only, but for people of both sexes, of all ages, and of every class.'

In April 1943, **Home Companion** pointed

▼ (and previous page) Members of the Women's Auxiliary Fire Service exercising, 1939. (Courtesy Catherine Gilman)

▶ This photograph from Health & Efficiency magazine of 1941 shows the idealised male body. Notice that the upper body is much worked on, but the legs are far less muscular than would be the case in his modern counterpart.

out that there was more to exercise than losing weight: *'There are some people who only think of exercise as a means of getting slimmer. This is, of course, all wrong. Swimming, which is one of the finest exercises known, is also the commonest one to be recommended to women who want to add to their bust measurements, and cycling is well known for improving the shape of the calf of the leg. The real beauty of regular exercise is that it should, by making you healthier, improve your figure – thinning away in some parts and developing in others.'*

Fresh air was important. Evelyn Forbes again: *'If you are to be healthy and beautiful, the blood must be air-conditioned. If you are air-starved your hair will be dank and lifeless, your eyes shadowed, your complexion pale and shabby, your figure puffy and overweight. This breathing exercise will slim the figure as well as oxygenate the system.*

'Face the open window, stand erect with the hands placed on the lower ribs. Breathe in through your nose, keeping your chest as still as possible, but feeling the lower ribs expanding under your hands. When they are fully expanded, let the breath out slowly, while pulling in the abdominal wall. Twelve deep breaths will take just two minutes.'

A healthy diet was also stressed: *'Now that synthetic beauty – the cunningly contrived corset, the heavy, concealing powder-base and flattering eye-shadow – is almost unobtainable, the true beauty which is based on health is more important than ever. First and foremost you and I must eat correctly. Eat something green and raw each day, preferably a large mixed salad, and one lightly cooked green veg-*

etable, and most of your beauty needs will be adequately provided for.' Evelyn Forbes, **Housewife**, August, 1943.

'Salads are nature's tonics and beauty foods. They put a sparkle in the eyes, gloss on the hair and spring in the step. They're doubly important now; they have not only to play their own good part, but take the place of fruit as well. A salad a day should be your rule; a good big plateful, not just a finicky spoonful or so!' **Food Facts,** May, 1943.

And it wasn't just what you ate or drank. **Housewife** magazine advised: *'Take your summer drinks or your glass of milk or water through a straw. This brings into play the delicate muscles in the cheeks and round the corners of the mouth, muscles which from lack of use are apt to grow flabby.'*

And the results of all this? Again, the **Home Companion**: *'"In which we curve" – that's what might be said of all the Women's Services, because Jill Tar and Land Girl Jane need bigger clothes! The buyer in the gown department of one of the big stores tells me that this is a fact. Early nights, good food and plenty of exercise in the fresh air are filling out those corners and the result is more attractive feminine figures.'*

'Slimming is dead as mutton and forty-odd is the usual measurement given by Service brides who plan rushed weddings and buy off-the-peg wedding dresses. The little thirty-six-inch-hip frock languishes in the show-cases. Nobody wants 'em. It's the forty-sizes that get snapped up every time. And isn't it a tribute to Lord Woolton [Minister of Food] – to think that in this our fourth year of war, we girls are putting on

weight? Going around looking like a hop pole just isn't smart. Victorian curves are the thing. So if, when you tot up your measurements, you arrive at a good figure, don't worry – you're in the fashion!'

However, many women did worry: *'I still get more letters from women who want to lose weight than from those who want to put it on. Dieting is obviously out of the question these days because each of us needs the basic ration. But reducing exercises are better today than they ever were, and if they're faithfully carried out they can work wonders with the lumpiest figure. Don't just do them once or twice and then forget about them, because, to be efficacious, they have to be done regularly over a considerable period of time. You didn't gain those extra ounces in a day, so it's a dead certainty you won't lose them all in a rush.*

'If your figure's in good trim you'll be able to save coupons on corsets and belts. We weren't meant to rely upon elastic and bone to keep our waistlines neat, because each of us is provided with a perfectly good belt of muscle, which, if used correctly and kept in condition, will give us a better figure than any belt. On the other hand, once allowed to get soft and flabby, they can ruin the lines of your most expensive frock.'

Corsets not only used coupons, (in 1941, girdles, roll-ons and corsets were three coupons, corselettes, covering both hips and bust, four), they also used a great deal of elastic. In 1942, Japanese advances in the Far East meant the loss of rubber from plantations in Malaya; one result of this was that elastic became very scarce. Elastic for knickers, suspender belts and for corsets was increasingly difficult to replace, although you might try to crochet gussets to replace the worn-out elastic panels in treasured foundation garments. [Roll-ons had disappeared along with stockings; being boneless, they were 'anchored down' by the stockings – without them they rode up.]

Good Housekeeping suggested massage as a means to the preferred shape: *'Let's take the legs first. Dust them with talc and, starting at the heel, pinch firmly up the back of the leg until you reach the inside of the knee. Do this as often as you can bear to, then, using both hands, massage from ankle to thigh*

with a firm, stroking movement. The pinching and stroking, if done alternately, make the process more bearable. This massage – don't ask me why – hurts less when done under water, so it's a good plan to do some part of your reducing drill in your bath. Do the rest, five minutes of it at a time, when putting on and taking off your stockings.

'The upper arms are made slim in much the same way and are pinched and slapped from elbow to shoulder. Grip your left arm with your right hand and twist the flesh away from the body. Start at the elbow and work towards the shoulder with an outward, semicircular movement, gripping, squeezing and twisting. Alternate stroking and slapping will also make this easier to bear. If you happen to have some Epsom salts, this will speed up the reduction. Take a handful of moistened salts in the palm of your hand and rub the skin with it while squeezing away the flesh. Rinse off the salts thoroughly, rub dry and apply a little hand lotion.'

One recurring theme was the effect of war work on the hands. One correspondent to **Home Companion** in September 1943, wrote: *'Mine is a pretty busy life as I'm doing a full-time job in a munitions factory ... my only worry is my hands, which used to be my pride and joy, are now becoming very work-weary looking. They're actually getting wrinkled and horny-looking and somehow I never manage to get them really clean.'*

'First and foremost, whenever you wash your hands, see that they are thoroughly well dried afterwards; otherwise they chap easily. Rinse them in cold or lukewarm water to close the pores. If you are doing work in the house, try to get into the habit of wearing gloves. You soon get used to them, and it prevents dirt from getting ingrained. Once a week, if you can manage to get a little oil, rub some in the palms and over the backs, and then wash in warm, soapy water. The oil helps to release any dirt and gives a lovely smooth effect after the washing is finished. Dry the hands, and then take a little skin food between the thumb and fingers of one and massage the knuckles of the other with a firm rotary movement, thumbs on top and fingers underneath ... never, never omit to cream the hands before going to bed. And then sleep in gloves, mitts made from a scrap of soft cotton will do excellently.'

Spirella perfects the modern "Juno"

◄ For most women, the foundation garment was a necessary part of dress. Rubber shortages meant that these became increasingly difficult to get.

To those of you who are not so slender comes Spirella to mould your figure on "Junoesque" lines. Your Spirella, designed in conformity with Nature's own laws of support and control, accomplishes the preservation or restoration of a perfect figure of womanly grace. The hands of the clock are set back. As your Spirella Corsetiere I am ready to attend you.

"I am Miss Spirella"

P.S.—Oh, by the by—You will find my address on the Spirella page of your TELEPHONE DIRECTORY

Spirella
individual corsetry service in your own home

In August 1944, **Home Chat** recommended that the 'holiday at home' should be seen as an opportunity to do something about one's hands: *Time and time again I've told you what miracles a 'pack works on your face and neck. Now, just for once let yourself be really extravagant and apply its magic to your hands, your arms. Give them a pack, lemon-magnesia, clasmic, just whatever you can discover. And if those are quite "off the market" in your district – try to get a small quota of fuller's earth. Mix it to a paste with a very little witch-hazel, and use as you would the pack.*

'Steam the hands and arms to open the pores, smooth on the pack paste and leave it to do its good work for fifteen minutes, then gently wash it off with luke-warm water. Now plunge arms and hands in a basin of cold, cold water, and finish up by massaging in a really generous application of hand cream.

'Or, another alternative, if pack and fuller's earth are both unobtainable, after the steaming process, cover arms and hands with cold cream, leave that on for ten minutes, and then wipe it off with a pad of cotton-wool moistened with cold water.'

Hands could be a problem for the young, too: *'Red hands are the bane of many young people, who get the habit of trying to hide them with awkward movements. The cause may be a thin skin and poor circulation, or some fault in diet, for this reason give the girl as much cheese, milk and fats as war-time diet allows, encourage her to do skipping or other exercise every day, and train her to give herself an all-over friction with a loofah or coarse towel during the bath. A whitening, softening hand-cream is a tremen-dous help, and if you'll encourage her to clean her fingernails with a soapy sponge and give them a simple buffer treatment every day.'* **Good Housekeeping**, February 1943.

During September 1939, among the inevitable wartime top-ics, debate raged in the

Daily Mirror's letters page over the propor-tions of the perfect female leg. The consensus was: ankle, 8 inches in circumference, calf, 14 inches, and thigh, 22 inches.

'Your feet are working harder today than ever before, but are you giving them any extra care? Few women do, and yet they're surprised when their long suffering feet let them down now and again. Remember pedicures and a nightly massage from toe to ankle will go a long way to keeping you on the road and to keeping your feet young in appearance as well as in action.' **Home Companion**, September 1943.

Tattoos in the 1940s were an overwhelm-ingly working-class, male, fashion. Sailors and soldiers, especially when overseas, often had a tattoo done. These military associations leant tattoos an air of masculinity, so that by the Second World War a large percentage of working-class males were tattooed. Men from the middle and upper classes who had tattoos had them mainly as souvenirs of service days. It was also not unknown for women to have tattoos. Originally they had been fairly common amongst prostitutes and fairground artistes, but during the inter-war years some of the more daring 'gay young things' had tattoos.

Tattoos were kept fairly discreet; men had them on the arms, high enough to be easily covered, sometimes on the chest and back. Tattoos on the hands and especially the face were rarities. Common designs were hearts and scrolls with names or slogans, 'death before dishonour' and 'Mum' or 'Mother'. Daggers featured, as did skulls, bluebirds and flowers. National symbols were common, and service related symbols, although commandos were advised against having any tattoos which might give them away should they be cut off while on a mission. It is also interest-ing that tattoos were rare in the RAF, perhaps because, being a new service, there was no tradition of tattooing. Perhaps due to this military association it was also not unknown for members of the women's auxiliary services to have tattoos done.

▼ A range of tattoos from a tattooist's sample sheet of the period. Note the various British themes, and the USA and USN (Navy) ones for American servicemen.

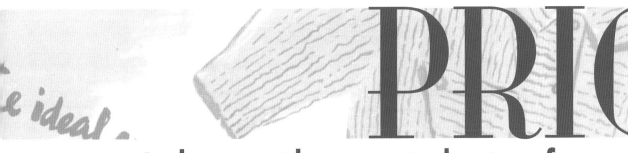

PRICE

A short guide to typical prices from the period

CLOTHES – MEN

General

Overcoat – 79/6, 16 coupons (1943)
Raincoat – 30/-, Military style 42/- (1940)
Trench Coat – 30/- (1939)
Cumberland tweed suit – £5. 17. 6 (1941)
Cumberland tweed jacket – £3. 15 (1941)
Worsted trousers – 16/-, 5 coupons (1941)
Viyella weekend shirt – 16/3 (plus tax) (1940)
Tunic shirt with two collars – 8/-, 7 coupons (1941)
Poplin Utility tunic shirts – 12/5, 7 coupons (1944)
Viyella socks – 2/6 (1939-40), 3/3 (1941)
Tie – 2 for 3/-, 2 coupons (1941)

Workwear

Heavy navy drill shirts – 9/-, 5 coupons (1941)
Boiler suit – 17/5, 4 coupons (1944)
Bib-and-brace – 8/4 to 10/6, no coupons, (1941) 10/10,
    3 coupons (1944)

Underwear

Merino mix: vests – 6/6, 4 coupons, full-length pants – 7/6,
    4 coupons (1941)
Interlock vests, half sleeves – 1/10, 2 coupons (1945)
Interlock pants ankle length – 2/3, 2 coupons (1945)

Nightwear

Wincyette Utility nightshirt – 13/8, 8 coupons (1944)
Winceyete Utility pyjamas – 11/8 to 14/4, 8 coupons (1944)

CLOTHES –WOMEN

Suits

Two piece suit – £4. 17. 6, 18 coupons (1943)
Rushweave Moyageshel – £5. 9. 1, 9 coupons (1944)
Tweed suit, Harris-type cloth – £4. 2. 2, 18 coupons (1945)

Coats

Mac – 13/-, 7 coupons to 14/6, 9 coupons (1941)
WX overcoat in tweed – 89/11 (1945)
Full length Indian lamb and ocelot seal – £70 (1945)
Full length, lamb, coney, moleskin, fox – £29 (1945)

Dresses

Art spun silk – 14/-, 7 coupons (1941)
Macclesfield silk dresses – from 64/6 (1942)
Heavy crepe – £13. 14. 2, 11 coupons (1942)
Rushweave Moyageshel – £4. 12. 1, 7 coupons (1944)
Macclesfield striped art silk – 77/6 (1944)
Printed crepe dress – £10. 1. 5, 7 coupons (1945)
Lightweight wool dress – £14.12. 6, 11 coupons (1945)
Print dress in art silk – £10, 19. 5, 7 coupons (1945)
Button-through frock, rayon – £9 15. 9, 7 coupons (1945)

Various

Art Silk jumper – 15/6, 5 coupons (1941)
WX jumper – 9/9, 5 coupons (1941)
Fleecy lined stockinette slacks – 10/6, 5 coupons (1941)
Skirts – 11/- to 12/6, 6 coupons (1941)
Blouses – 3/6 to 5/-, 4 coupons (1941)

Maternity wear

Frocks – 27/11 (1939), 31/6 (1940)
Dress, printed crepe – 5½ gns (1942)
Dress, woollen – 6 gns (1943)
Suit, wool – £7. 13. 7 (1944)

Working clothes

Cross-over overalls – 2/3, o/s, 2/7 (1939)
Cross-over overalls – 4/3, 6 coupons (1941)
Bib & brace overalls – 12/-, no coupons (1941)
Mill style overall – 4/6, 6 coupons (1941)
Overalls, blue or green – 11/1 (1944)
Wrap-over coat – 9/10, 3 coupons (1944)
Afternoon apron – 2/3, 3 coupons (1941)
Pinarette – 3/1, o/s, 3/7 (1944)

Underwear

Combinations, interlock – 4/-, 4 coupons (1941), o/s, 9/3, 6 coupons (1944)
Knickers, Viscana (Directoire or French) – from 2/6 (1939)
Rayon locknit – 2/6, o/s, 2/11 (August 1939) 2/9, o/s, 3/3 (December 1939)
Art silk – 3/6, o/s, 4/6 (1939)
Rayon – 3/9, 3 coupons, o/s, 4/3, 1/2, 3 coupons (1944)
Wool – 4/9, 3 coupons, o/s, 5/6, 3 coupons (1944)
Viscana panties – from 2/6 (1939)
Viscana cami-Knickers – from 5/- (1939)
Viscana slips – from 5/- (1939)
Viscana vests – from 2/6 (1939)
Interlock vests – 2/- (1945)
Brassiere, broche – 2/3, 1 coupon (1941), crossover, satin – 4/3, 1 coupon (1941)
Winceyette nightdress – o/s 7/-, 6 coupons (1941)
Cotton interlock pyjamas – 8/6, 8 coupons (1941)

Foundation garments

Corsets, Silkese foundations – 30/- (1940), 35/9 (1942)
Maternity corsets – 5/3 (1940)
Ambrose Wilson corselette – 9/11 (1939)
Girdle, art silk brocade – 4/3, 3 coupons (1941)
Elastic roll-on – 4/3, 3 coupons (1941)

CLOTHES –
CHILDREN

Babies

Locknit rompers – 4/9, (1941)
Pram sets – 6/- to 11/-, 2 to 3 coupons (1941)
Pilch knickers – 1/- pair, 1 coupon (1941)
Jersey suit – 3/6 (1941)
Legging set – 1/-, 4 to 8 coupons (1941)

Girls

Double-breasted overcoat of pilot cloth, lined – 33in, 21/-, to 46in, 35/- (1939)
Coats – from 48/7 (1945), mackintoshes – 8/-, to 9/-, (1939)
Raincoats – from 42/1 (1945)
Gym slip – 9/- to 11/-, 3 coupons (1941)
Gym tunics – from 15/6 (1945)
Blazers – 13/- (1939), from 15/3 (1945)
Blouses – from 9/8 (1945)
Kilt – 3/9, 6 coupons (1941)
Party frock for the older girl in art silk – 8/- to 9/-, 5 coupons (1941)
Fleecy-lined knickers – 1/3 to 1/6 (1939)
Fleecy knickers – 1/3 to 1/2d, 1 coupon (1945)
Guide tunic – 3/6 to 5/- (1939)

Boys

Blazer suit – 11/-, 5 coupons, to 12/6, 9 coupons (1941)
Tweed suits – from 76/5 (1945)
All-wool flannel suits – from 36/9 (1945)
Overcoat – 20/-, 6 coupons, to 24/- 10 coupons (1941)
Trench coats – from 49/2 (1945)
Mac – 10/6, 4 coupons to 12/6, 7 coupons (1941)
Flannelette shirts – 4/6 to 4/9, 4 coupons (1941)
Grey flannel shirts, collar attached – from 7/- (1945)
Interlock vests – 1/1, 1 coupon (1945)
Winter underwear – from 4/9 (1945)
Trunks, interlock – 1/3, 1/2, 1 coupon (1945)

HANDS & FEET

Men's Shoes

Portland shoes – 26/11 to 33/6 (1941)
Oxford shoes in leather – 17/6, 7 coupons (1941)
Oxford shoes in suedette – 8/6, 7 coupons (1941)
Waukeezi – 37/6 to 50/- (1942)
Football boots – 15/-, 4 coupons 1941)
Leather slippers, fleecy lining – 7/6 to 8/6, 4 coupons (1941)

Women's Shoes

Eve-rest – from 17/11 (1940)
Norvic suede – 19/11 (1940)
Oxford shoes – 9/6, 5 coupons (1941)
Suedette brogues – 9/-, 5 coupons (1941)
Brown Gibson with low leather heel – 29/3 (1942)
Utility, suede, side lace – 28/1 (1942)
Devonshire gusset court shoe – 22/10 (1944)

Children's Shoes

Girls' school shoes – 6/6 to 7/3, 1 to 2 coupons (1941)
Boys' derby shoes – 9/3 to 10/3, 1 to 2 coupons (1941)
Children's sandals – 3/6 to 4/3, 1 to 2 coupons (1941)
Plimsolls, sizes 10 to 2 – 1/6, 3 to 8 – 2/- (1939)
Wellington boots, sizes 3 to 8 – 6/6 (August 1939),
    7/- (December 1939)

Socks

Men's cashmere socks – 2/4 pair, 3 coupons (1941)
Men's cotton half-hose – 3 pairs, 1/9, 3 coupons (1941)

Stockings

Black or brown lisle – 2/3 (1939)
Black or brown sea island cotton – 3/- (1939)
Brown cashmere – 2/3 (1939)

Hats & Gloves

Rubberised ivory Batiste pixie hood – 1/8 (1941)
Men's trilby hat in Air Force blue, navy, brown or grey –
8/- (1941)
Women's brown leather gloves – 7/-, 2 coupons (1941)
Men's tan cape gloves – 9/-, 2 coupons (1941)
Boys' brown leather gloves – 6/6, 2 coupons (1941)
Motor cyclists' gauntlets – 8/6, 2 coupons (1941)

ACCESSORIES

Wedding Rings

Ciro, gold band – 12/6 (1940)
Ciro, diamonds in solid gold and platinette – 25/- (1940)
Bravingtons, solid gold court shape – 25/- (1944)
Bravingtons, solid gold fancy shape – 29/9 (1944)

Wristwatches

Benson's, Gent's 9ct gold – £7. 10. 0, silver, £4. 7. 6 (1939)
Accurist, Gent's 9ct gold – £15. 19. 6, luminous dial,
    5/- extra (1945)
Accurist, Ladies' 9ct gold – £14. 2. 6, luminous dial,
    5/- extra (1945)

Cases

Attaché case, fibre – 16in, 10/3 (1945)
Suitcase, fibre, 1 lock, 2 straps – 26in, 35/3 (1945)

Umbrellas

Ladies' oiled finished umbrella in natural, red, navy and
    green – 10/- (1941)
Men's black rolling umbrella – 11/6 (1941)

Material

Sparno-crease, Sparva-Spun, Sparvasylk, Sparva-lin –
    36in wide, 1/- yard (1939)
Pure Irish dress linen (Coloured) – 36in, med. wt, 5/6 yd
    (1941)
All wool tweed – 54in wide, 11/6 yard (1942)
Cotton fabric – 36in wide, 1/9 to 2/7, 1/5 yd, 2 coupons
(1944)
Dayella printed – 36in wide, 5/5 yd, 3 coupons (1944)

Utility Lingerie crepe – 36in wide, 3/11 yd, 2 coupons (1944)
Utility Lingerie satin – 36in wide, 4/6 yd, 2 coupons (1944)
Utility Rayon – 36in wide, 3/11 yard, 2 coupons (1943)

Wool

3 and 4-ply fingering – 5$\frac{1}{2}$ oz (1939)
Double knitting and 4-ply fingering wool in 3lb packets in
    Navy, Army and Air Force colours – 4/6lb (1939)
Super Botany wool – 5d oz (1939)
Viyella yarn – 9$\frac{1}{2}$oz. (1940)
Angel skin yarn – 1/4 oz (1941)
Rayon Crepe – 2/5$\frac{1}{2}$, 4oz (1941)
Spun Silk – 1/8 oz (1941)
Specially fine 2 ply – 1/11, 2oz (1941)
Patons Beehive fingering 2, 3 & 4-ply & baby wool cream,
    sky and pink – 9$\frac{1}{2}$oz, 2oz, 1 coupon (1944)

COSMETICS & TOILETRIES

Coty Four Seasons Eau de Cologne – 2/- to 27/6 (1940)
Coty perfume – 3/9 to 11 gns (1939)
Goya perfume – £3. 10. 0 (1944)
Anne French Cleansing Milk – 1/6 and 3/6 (1939)
Icilma Foundation Vanishing Cream – 10$\frac{1}{2}$d to 3/6 (1945)
Nivea tubes & jars – 6d to 1/9 (1940)
Odo-ro-no – 6d to 1/6 (1939)
Pond's cold cream – 6d to 5/- (1940)
Reudel bath cubes – 2d (1939)
Tangee rouge – 7$\frac{1}{2}$d to 4/3 (1942)
Veet hair remover – 1/3 to 2/6 (1939)
Yardley Lavender perfume – 2/6 to 42/-, talc 1/2 and 2/6,
Lavendomeal – 3/-, 5/6, 9/6; gift cases – 2/6 to 45/-
    (1939)

Face Powder

Pond's in 6 shades – 6d, 1/-, 1/9 (1939-40)
Coty airspun – 1/3 box, 2/3 (1940)
Max Factor, Pan Cake refills – 7/4 (1945)
Goya – 10/9 (1944)

Lipstick

Outdoor Girl – 6d, 1/-, and 2/6 (1939)
Guitar – 2/-, 4/6, 6/6; refills – 1/3, 3/- (1939-40)
Goya – 7/6 (1944)
Tangee, refills – 1/6, 4/3 (1940-early 1942), 1/10, 5/-
    (October 1942-March 1943), 2/1, 5/10 (June 1943-
    April 1944)

Nail varnish

Amami nail varnish – 6d (1940)
Cutex nail polish – 9d, 1/6 (1939)

Soap

Eve toilet soap – 2d (1939), 3d (1941), 3d, 1 coupon
    (1942-43) 3$\frac{1}{2}$d, 1 coupon (1944)
Knight's Castile – 4d (1939)
Lifebuoy Toilet Soap, new handy tablet – 3d (1941)
Lux – 3d (1939)
Palmolive – 3d (1940)
Pears Original Transparent – 4$\frac{1}{2}$d (1939)
Wright's Coal Tar – 6d tablet (1939)
Yardley Lavender, three tablets – 2/6 (1939)

Toothpaste

Colgate – 6d, 10$\frac{1}{2}$d, and 1/6 (1940)
Eucryl tooth power – 3d to 1/- (1940), 9d to 1/3 (1945)
Gibb's SR – 6d, 1/3 (1939)
Macleans tooth paste, one size during war – 1/1 tube (1945)

Denture Powder

Milton – 6d, 1/-, 1/9 (1939), 1/3 and 2/2 a bottle
    (1944-45)
Steradent – 1/- and 1/9 tins (1940)
Kolynos Denture Fixative – 1/3 and 3/3 (1942-44)

Toothbrushes

Halex – 6d to 2/- (1939), 1/- plus tax, nylon bristles, 1/6
    plus tax (1941)
Meritor – 1/- to 2/5 (1941)
Tex, bristles – 2/- plus tax 5d, nylon – 1/8 plus tax 4d (1943)

Hands

Cutex hand cream – 2/- jar (1940)
Glymel hand cream – tubes 6d and 1/-, jars 2/6 (1939)
Snowfire Hand Jelly – tubes 3d, 6d, 1/- (1940)

Shampoo

Like most other goods, shampoo went up in price, but the war had another effect on many items which had been sold in several sizes. Standardisation meant that by 1944, only one size was available.
Amami – 3d, 6d (1939-40), 4d and 7^1/$_2$d (1941-43), 4d (1944-45)
Drene – 6d, 1/6, 2/6 (1939)
Eve – 2d (1939), 2^1/$_2$d (1940), 3d (1941-44)

Hair dressing

Amami Brilliantine – 6d (1939), 7^1/$_2$d (1941)
Pears solid brilliantine – 1/3 (Dec 39)
Amami Wave Set – standard 6d (1939), 7^1/$_2$d (1941), 9d (1943), 10^1/$_2$d (1944), spiritous – 1/3 (1939), 1/6 (1941), 1/10 (1943), 2/1^1/$_2$d (1944)
Brycreem – 1/- tubes, bottles 1/-, 1/6, 1/9, 2/6 (1940)
Petrol Hahn – 5/- and 7/6 a bottle inc. tax (1943)
Vaseline Hair Tonic – 1/6, 2/6, 3/- (1940)

At the hairdressers

Hair cut – 1/- (1941)
Shampoo and set – 2/6 (1941), 4/6 (1943)
Marcel Wave – 3/- (1941)
Permanent Wave – 15/- to 30/- (1941)
Halo sleeping cap – cotton 1/-, art silk 1/6, lace 1/11 (1940) in 6 pastel shades and all forces colours 1/11 (1941)
Halo art silk hair nets – in all natural hair and 6 pastel shades 2d (1940)

Shaving soap

Coro-Shave – tubes 1/3 and 7^1/$_2$d, jars – 1/9 and 1/- (1941)
Colgate brushless shave cream – 6d, 1/-, 1/6 (1939), 1/6 and 2/6 inc. tax (1944)
Jif shaving stick – 6d (1939), cream 6d and 1/- (1940)
Rolls – sticks 2/6 (Refils 1/6), bowls 3/6 (Refils 1/6), (1939)

Razors

Ever-Ready – 10/6 (1939)
Remington electric – £3. 17. 6 (1939)
Rolls Razor – 21/- to 27/6 (1939)
Wilkinson – 7/6 to 21/1 (1939)

Razor Blades

Eclipse – 5 for 1/8 (1940), 3d each inc. purchase tax (1942-45)
Gilette – Thin, 1/3, six, Blue – 1/3, five, Stainless – 1/8, five (1941), 2d each (1945)

BIBLIOGRAPHY

Books

Joanna Chase, *Sew and Save*, (the Literary Press Ltd, 1941)
Richmal Crompton, *William and the Evacuees* (George Newnes Ltd, 1940)
Richmal Crompton, *William Does his Bit* (George Newnes Ltd, 1941)
Fougasse, *The Changing face of Britain* (Methuen, 1940)
Catherine Franks, *The Pictorial Guide to Modern Home Dressmaking* (Odhams Press Ltd, 1940)
Charles Graves, *Women in Green* (Heinemann Ltd, 1948)
Caroline Haslett, *Munition Girl* (English Universities Press, 1942)
Norman Longmate, *How We Lived Then* (Hutchinson, 1971)
Dr Harry Roberts, *Keep Fit in Wartime* (Watts & Co, 1940)
Sillince, *United Notions* (Collins, 1943)
Sillince, *We're Still All in It* (Collins, 1942)
Donald Thomas, *An Underworld at War* (John Murray, 2003)
E. S. Turner, *The Phoney War on the Home Front* (The Quality Book Club, 1961)
Citizens at War and After (Harrap, 1945)
Civilian Supplies in Wartime Britain (Ministry of Information, 1945)
Gifts you can make yourself (Odhams Press, 1944)
Instructions for American Servicemen in Britain (written in 1942 – Bodleian Library, 1994)
Knitted Garments for All (Odhams Press, 1944)
Knitting Illustrated (Odhams Press, 1948)
Make Do and Mend (Ministry of Information, 1943)
Meet the Common People (The Studio Publications, 1943)
Modern Publicity in Wartime (The Studio Publications, 1941)
Modern Knitting Illustrated (Odhams Press, 1940)
The Pictorial Guide to Modern Home Knitting (Odhams Press, 1939)
Pierced Hearts and True Love (Derek Verschoyle Ltd, 1953)
Practical Home Knitting (Odhams Press, 1949)
Practical Knitting Illustrated (Odhams Press, 1940)
ed. Judy Attfield *Utility Reassessed* (Manchester University Press, 1999)
ed. Tom Harrisson *Utility Furniture and Fashion 1941 to 1951* (I.L.E.A., 1974)
ed. Tom Harrisson *War Factory – Mass Observation report* (Victor Gollancz, 1943)
The War Time Lawyer (Daily Express, 1940)
War Time Needlework (Daily Express, 1940)

Pamphlets, etc.

101 ways to save money in wartime (National Savings Movement)
The Clothing Coupon Quiz (HMSO, 1941)
The 1942 Clothing Coupon Quiz (HMSO, 1942)
Food Facts (The Ministry of Food)
Health for A.R.P. Workers (Central Council for Health Education)
Knitting for the RAF (Raphael Tuck, 1939)
Make Do and Mend leaflets (Board of Trade)
The Market Square (HMSO, 1944)
The Sixit Club (autumn, 1941)

Periodicals

The Daily Mirror
Everywoman
Good Housekeeping
Health & Efficiency
Home Chat
Home Companion
Home Notes
Housewife
The Illustrated London News
The Jeweller and Metalworker
The Kentish Mercury
The Lady's Companion
The Listener
London Opinion
Modern Woman
Mother
Mother and Home
My Weekly
The Optician
Picture Post
Stitchcraft
The Sunday Pictorial
The Tatler
The Tailor and Cutter
Woman
Woman & Beauty
Woman & Home
Woman's Own
Woman's Weekly

INDEX